T0013193

DRINK *like a* LOCAL

AUSTIN

*A Field Guide to
Austin's Best Bars*

Drink Like a Local: Austin
A Field Guide to Austin's Best Bars

Copyright © 2023 by Cider Mill Press Book Publishers LLC.

This is an officially licensed book by Cider Mill Press Book Publishers LLC. All rights reserved under the Pan-American and International Copyright Conventions.

No part of this book may be reproduced in whole or in part, scanned, photocopied, recorded, distributed in any printed or electronic form, or reproduced in any manner whatsoever, or by any information storage and retrieval system now known or hereafter invented, without express written permission of the publisher, except in the case of brief quotations embodied in critical articles and reviews.

The scanning, uploading, and distribution of this book via the internet or via any other means without permission of the publisher is illegal and punishable by law. Please support authors' rights, and do not participate in or encourage piracy of copyrighted materials.

13-Digit ISBN: 978-1-64643-350-6
10-Digit ISBN: 1-64643-350-5

This book may be ordered by mail from the publisher. Please include $5.99 for postage and handling. Please support your local bookseller first!

Books published by Cider Mill Press Book Publishers are available at special discounts for bulk purchases in the United States by corporations, institutions, and other organizations. For more information, please contact the publisher.

Cider Mill Press Book Publishers
"Where good books are ready for press"
501 Nelson Place
Nashville, Tennessee 37214

cidermillpress.com

Typography: Ballinger, Condor, Pacifico, Poppins, Stolzl

Printed in Malaysia

23 24 25 26 27 OFF 5 4 3 2 1
First Edition

DRINK *like a* LOCAL
AUSTIN

A Field Guide to Austin's Best Bars

VERONICA MEEWES

CIDER MILL PRESS

BOOK PUBLISHERS

CONTENTS

What does it mean to "drink like a local"? That's a question I was often asked while writing this book, and one I found myself pondering quite frequently. First, you have to define "local," and in a city that is said to gain nearly 200 new residents each day, that definition would vary greatly, depending on who you asked.

I too am a transplant, but I just happened to precede the masses. When I got here in 2005, Austin still had a sleepy small-town feel but more than enough entertainment for this East Coaster's insatiable need for discovery and diversion. There was a tangible cowboy-hippie vibe to the place —thanks to The Armadillo World Headquarters for setting that precedent. Much like our spirit animal, Matthew McConaughey, Austin was effortlessly cool. And it felt like the eccentric and the unexpected were not only accepted, but encouraged. Of course, my predecessors were quick to let me know how much it had already changed, and I soon learned that this city suffers from that affliction. (The one where, no matter when you moved here, it was better before you arrived.)

Interestingly enough, during my research I came across a letter sent to the American-Statesman in 1884, penned by an Austin resident who went by "Old Citizen." His letter expressed urgent concern over the buildings at 6th and Brazos being cleared to make way for the Driskill Hotel. "One by one the old landmarks leave us and but few of the original houses of Austin remain," he lamented. It was really eye-opening to see that Austinites have been resistant to change since... well, since the city first started.

But these days, Austin's growth is a hot-button issue, and for good reason. This city, like so many before it, is being drastically reshaped by gentrification, fueled in big part by the many tech companies that have established hubs here in the last decade. At its worst, the Californication of Austin is pricing out established locals from their neighborhoods. And when the demographics and cultural landscape of a city change, its businesses are directly affected too. Austin's dives and blue-collar hangouts are an endangered species, and many have been forced to either shut their doors or adapt to a different Austin. Growth has brought luxury condos and strict noise ordinances to places that have historically been live music districts. Sometimes it feels like this version of our city is designed for the bachelor and bachelorette parties that descend upon it in droves and take to the streets by pedal-powered pub crawls. Austin, once the effortless cool kid, seems like it's lost its sense of self; these days, those tie-dye "Keep Austin Weird" T-shirts are more of a plea than a motto.

As a writer, I've often worried that I am a part of the "problem." In fact, I know I am. I've written Austin guides that have appeared in national publications, and countless roundups shared across social media, that undoubtedly helped spur interest in this city. In fact, I had a good friend beg me not to include one of his favorite bars in this book, and I really thought about it long and hard before I did—sorry Buster, but The Silver Medal is too good to leave out! You see, growth is inevitable, so let's teach the new-comers to drink like locals. Let's cherish the places that capture the true Austin, whether they opened in 1962 or 2002.

Of course, I couldn't include all the bars I wanted to, and there will be new ones open by the time this book is published. Think of this as a love letter to a city in flux. You'll find dives layered with history right along-side next-level cocktail bars. You'll discover neighborhood taverns that are fixtures of the community in ways that transcend the physical walls. You'll learn about places to make new friends or catch up with old ones;

to watch the game or wait for election results to roll in; to celebrate, to mourn, and to be a part of a community. Because, if you didn't already know it, the pandemic certainly showed us that bars are about so much more than drinking. They have the power to bring people together, to find common ground, to provide a safe space. And that has possibly never been more important than it is right now.

Whether you grew up here or just arrived, welcome! I'm happy to report that the spirit of Austin is still alive and well. You just need to know where to look for it.

BRENTWOOD, CRESTVIEW, AND WOOTEN

It seems like no neighborhood is immune to Austin's rapid growth. Thankfully, the soul of old Austin can still be found in certain neighborhoods—and the stretch of Burnet Road between Koenig Lane and 183 is one of them. Brentwood, Crestview, and Wooten, which blend together quite seamlessly, are three family-friendly residential neighborhoods stacked on top of each other, just east of Burnet. The tree-lined side streets east of Burnet are filled with a mix of original single-family bungalows and new modern builds. Luxury condo developments keep creeping further up Burnet itself, while trendy restaurants follow like DipDipDip Tatsu-ya, Bufalina Due, and Barley Swine—and they are all fantastic, for the record. However, the city's eccentric spirit is kept alive, thanks to vintage neon signs, multiple thrift and consignment stores, and some of the city's best dive bars, like Buddy's Place (page 12), The Aristocrat Lounge (page 15), and The Little Longhorn Saloon (page 22). While you're in the hood, soak up those drinks with a burger and onion rings from Top Notch Hamburgers, the iconic drive-in made famous by its appearance in hometown hero Richard Linklater's *Dazed and Confused*.

BUDDY'S PLACE

8619 Burnet Road
Austin, TX 78757

As dive bars—and their working-class clientele—get pushed further outside of central Austin, Buddy's Place remains one of the last ones standing—nay, thriving. And sure, you could call many of the bars in this book a dive bar— it depends on your definition of such a watering hole, really. But Buddy's Place is really the platonic ideal of a dive bar.

The building itself has been a bar since the 1950s and the entire place seems to be frozen in the 1990s, which is when Buddy Lamb and his partner Jackie Smith took it over and named it Buddy's Place; in 1996 to be exact, and they have the carpeting to prove it. The walls are plastered with beer ads and neon signs, plus framed photos of Lamb and Smith with patrons over the years. Card tables and captain's mate chairs line the perimeter, all facing the two centerpiece pool tables [which are free on Mondays and just 75 cents a game otherwise]. A row of cushioned bar stools face the well-worn wooden bar, where a line-up of hanging bottles and cans showcases the beer selections; Budweiser and Miller Light are the best sellers, and you won't find any craft beer here. There's even a creepily lifelike mannequin sitting at one of the tables, usually donning a cowboy hat—or an elf hat, if it's Christmastime.

"That's Jasper—he gets more action than any other guy in this bar," assures Shana Laney. "More women take pictures with him and kiss him than anyone else

in here!" She then starts regaling me with stories about where she and the other bartenders have hidden Jasper to scare each other through the years. The jukebox soundtrack seamlessly moves from Conway Twitty to Alan Jackson to Dwight Yoakam. "We have both kinds of music—country and western," she says matter-of-fact-ly.

Laney has worked in the industry for over 20 years, and behind the bar at Buddy's for 16 of those years. She started working here in 2007, and dated Smith for seven of those years. When Lamb passed away, Smith ran it until his passing in 2016. A regular named Duane Johnson then bought the bar from Smith's kids, promising to run it exactly as Smith would have wanted. He now owns two-thirds of the bar and the other third belongs to Wyatt Earp Smith, Smith's 12-year-old dog who can usually be found holding court in a little gray bed behind the bar.

Like any good dive bar worth its salt, Buddy's Place has some steadfast regulars. One of them, 94-year-old Chester, gets dropped off every day by his daughter on her way to work, and he even has a chair with his name printed on it. "You're allowed to sit there but if Chester walks in, you need to get the fuck up," says Laney. "He was sitting here when JFK was assassinated, to let you know how long he's been coming here."

Buddy's is also one of the only places in town where you can still bring in your own bottle of liquor and buy "set-ups" from the bar. However, the bottle can only be shared with the people in your party— passing it around the bar would result in immediate ejection. The biggest change that's been made at Buddy's is in the space where local bands play on Wednesday through Friday for tips. During the pandemic, they created a bandstand for the performers and put railings up to create an official dancefloor. As a result, the iconic shuffleboard had to be removed, though it is still advertised on the blue-paint-ed brick facade, along with "pool, darts and sports TV." There is also a stencil of John Wayne with the words "Welcome Pilgrim," and red letters spelling out "Buddy's Place: Home of Happiness."

"It's called the Home of Happiness for a reason," says Laney. "Because we are literally a giant family."

Visit when they open at noon and the space, which gets quite dark at night, will be flooded with sunshine through the propped-open front door. The regulars stationed at the bar will beckon you to have a seat and welcome you right into the conversation. Buddy's Place still stands as a reminder that you don't need much to be a great bar: just good music, good people, and cold, cheap beer.

THE ARISTOCRAT LOUNGE

6507 Burnet Road
Austin, TX 78757

The Aristocrat Lounge may have changed hands and names in recent years, but it still maintains the integrity of the blue-collar neighborhood bar that welcomed Brentwood locals for 50 years. The Poodle Dog Lounge opened on Burnet Road in 1964 as a beer-only lounge where patrons could bring their own liquor and kill several hours playing pool and smoking cigs [which they allowed for years after the city's 2005 smoking ban].

Bar veterans Randall and Donya Stockton [who opened Beerland on Red River and revamped Rio Rita on East 6th Street in the early aughts] purchased the building from the last owner in 2014. Stockton had grown up watching NASCAR with his dad at the Poodle Dog, and didn't change much about it outside of obtaining a liquor license, giving the place a fresh coat of paint and adding a few fitting decor details. Musician Austin Kalman [guitarist for Austin-based band called Lions] ran The Aristocrat as opening manager before taking over operations entirely seven months prior to the pandemic. These days, you'll see more pints of local craft beer being consumed here than Schlitz. But don't let the name [or the vintage glass chandeliers] fool you. This is one of

the few bars in town where you can still find a cocktail for under $10.

"People always ask if [the name of the bar] is a reference to the joke, but it's not," says Austin. "I feel like Randall and Donya always had a real working class solidarity and punk DIY attitude and that carried over into the concept being a bit of an ironic jab."

Framed black and white photos of Marilyn Monroe left-over from the Poodle Dog days, line the perimeter and mounted deer heads peer down into dark green booths. Two huge red circular booths beckon larger parties to tuck in and enjoy chicken porridge and beef panang curry from Yeni's Fusion, the remarkable Indonesian food truck parked outside the front entrance. The bar's original shuffleboard still stretches across the back wall, and red felted pool tables are lit aglow by the retro green lamps above each one. Locals love coming for free pool on Tuesdays and Wednesdays, but Kalman says it's the friendly neighborhood vibe that keeps them coming back.

"I'm not a fan of hustle culture," says Austin. "We just take our time and have fun. So I think people come here for the relaxed, welcoming atmosphere. What is a dive bar anyway? It's just a bar full of regulars."

FIG HOT TODDY

"My Mamaw always had preserved and dried figs around when I was growing up in southeast Texas, so I find myself returning to them again and again as an ingredient," says Kalman. He originally created this Mission fig-infused bourbon for a take on an Old Fashioned called a Mission Statement [still one of their top sellers]. "But we crush it with the Infused Hot Toddy for the approximately 2½ weeks a year that it's actually cold here," he laughs. "There's just something about the warmth of Mission figs that really rounds out the other components."

1½ oz. Mission Fig-infused Bourbon

1 oz. House Toddy Syrup

2-4 dash Angostura bitters

Hot water

1. Combine bourbon, syrup, and bitters in 8-10 oz. mug with a cinnamon stick.
2. Add very hot water and stir before serving.

Mission Fig-infused Bourbon: Slice 3 to 4 oz. dried organic mission figs and combine with 1 liter bourbon [they use local Still Austin Straight Bourbon, but Old Grand-Dad works great too]. Let sit 24-36 hours, shaking occasionally. Strain.

House Toddy Syrup: Combine 2 lemons and 1 orange [quartered] with 4 cinnamon sticks in a pot with 500ml honey and 500ml water. Bring to a boil, then let simmer 15-20 mins. Let cool and strain.

LALA'S LITTLE NUGGET

2207 Justin Lane
Austin, TX 78757

It's always Christmas at Lala's Little Nugget, a Crestwood dive bar that remains trimmed and twinkling with yuletide cheer all year long. There are several theories as to how the Christmas bar came about. Some say the original owner Frances Lala's son died in Vietnam, and she just never took the ornaments down when he never made it home for Christmas. Others say her husband left right before Christmas, sending her into a depression, so she never got around to undecorating. When she resurfaced months later, the unintentional theme had taken off so she left them up. And in the least heart-wrenching of the rumors, she simply felt the bar looked too barren once she took down the Christmas decor, so she put it back up.

"It's whichever one you want it to be!" says co-owner Max Moreland, who knows the real story but won't give it up. "We let people decide for themselves."

Lala opened her eponymous Justin Lane strip mall tavern in October 1972, and worked there for the next 43 years. The only beer on draft was ZeigenBock and she sold overpriced pours of cheap Christian Brothers brandy, but whipped up a mean Bloody Mary. The place was always filled with cigarette smoke (long past the indoor smoking ban), but it was just the tax you paid to hang

out at this Lone Star North Pole. And Lala sure could be surly, despite the sugarplummy ambiance.

"Mean as a whip," laughs Moreland. "She didn't put up with any shit. There's stories of, like, a big strapping 25-year-old putting his cigarette out on the pool table and she'd go up and grab him by the ear and drag him right out the door."

In 2015, at age 84, Lala began to fall ill and she put the building up for sale. FBR Management, a group known for its preservation of iconic Austin bars like Star Bar (page 164) and Mean-Eyed Cat (page 179), acquired it. As with all the preservation projects they take on, FBR wanted to change as little as possible. Instead, they just enhanced the long-running Christmas theme by adding even more decorations.

"I said, 'If we're going to do this, I want Christmas to throw up in here,'" Moreland recalls.

The reindeer-led sleigh that used to stretch across the glowing sign outside has been upgraded to a bigger fleet, now prancing on the rooftop of a screened-in patio. Jeff Truth's mural of Willie Nelson as Kris Kringle greets guests as they arrive. Inside, even more oversized ornaments and nutcrackers hang from the green, red, and white tiled ceiling. Tinsel shimmers under twinkling strands of lights and the glow of chandeliers crafted from wagon wheels. The holly-berry red walls are filled with framed Christmas memorabilia, vintage photos, cross stitch Santas and old Armadillo Christmas Bazaar flyers. A railing around the entire space, just under the ceiling, displays an entire world of figurines and an impressive snow globe collection. Moreland says much of the decor has been donated by patrons and neighbors through the years.

"A lot of it is, sadly, from when a parent or grandparent passes away," he says. "It means a lot to us that they include us in that, and then they become a part of the bar."

Nowadays, there's eight beer taps and a short list of cocktails that rotate seasonally—but nothing too fancy because Lala wouldn't want that!—and the original Bloody Mary recipe remains untouched. Brooklyn Pie Co. serves New York style pies, calzones, and wings out of the kitchen too, so you can feel free to settle in and stay awhile for a game of foosball.

"As a midwestern, I think it feels like Grandma's base-ment," says Moreland. "It's warm, comforting and welcoming. It reminds me of home and community and I think people get that feeling when they walk in."

GRANDMA'S BOOZY EGG NOG

Lala's only served beer and wine for the first 43 years of its life. But as soon as they secured a liquor license in 2015, they began serving Grandma's Boozy Egg Nog during the holiday season. The recipe was passed down from bartender Peyton Giles-Nelson, who got the recipe from her 5th generation Texan MeMa. "While I can't reveal the secret recipe of the non-boozy eggnog, I can attest that any locally sourced eggnog will do the trick," says general manager Sunny Allen.

½ oz. brandy

½ oz. whiskey

½ oz. silver rum

½ oz. butterscotch liqueur/ schnapps

2-4 oz. eggnog (depending on how strong you want it to taste)

Spoonful of vanilla ice cream

1 dash nutmeg, to garnish

1 dash cinnamon, to garnish

1. Pour all ingredients into a shaker and shake for a few seconds until frothy.
2. Strain into a glass over ice.
3. Garnish with the cinnamon and/or nutmeg.

THE LITTLE LONGHORN SALOON

5434 Burnet Road
Austin, TX 78756

"**A**lright, here are the rules: don't act like an ass-hole, no shakin' the cage, no drinks on the cage. One shit and one shit only!" A petite girl with a powerful voice makes this announcement while cradling two hens in her bell-sleeved arms. She releases Tammy Wynette and Patsy Cline (yes, those are the birds' names) into a pen and they begin to stroll across numbered squares, pecking at feed. I hear voices all around me intermingled with the country music from inside seeping out into the parking lot:

"Oh here we go again."

"Come on, 35!"

"If it shit right now, I'd be happy."

"Blow on her butt!" the guy next to me yells over the crowd. When I laugh out loud, he says with a shrug, "What? It works!" We're standing around wishing and hoping for two chickens to poop on our lottery numbers: it can only be Chicken Shit Bingo at The Little Longhorn Saloon, the orange-and-white steepled bar on Burnet Road.

Dick Setliff originally opened Dick's Little Longhorn Saloon in 1963, and hired Ginny Kalmbach as a waitress. When Setliff died in 1993, he bequeathed the bar to her, and Dick's Little Longhorn Saloon became Ginny's Little Longhorn Saloon. Kalmbach, who had grown up on classic country music, decided to turn the tiny bar into a honky-tonk, despite its size limitations, hosting both local and touring musicians every night of the week. In 2000, country legend Dale Watson, who played his

very first gig at Ginny's, approached Kalmbach with an idea he had, based on a game of Cow Shit Bingo he'd experienced in California, and suggested they try to replicate the game with chickens instead to ramp up business on Sunday. Watson, who also became a partner in the bar for a period of time, is also responsible for the steeple on the bar. Contrary to popular belief, it wasn't a church in its past life; the spire was an addition he made after agreeing to officiate a wedding there.

When Kalmbach retired in 2013, Terry Gaona, who had also started as a bartender at Ginny's, and her husband David took over the bar and it then became simply The Little Longhorn Bar. In the next few years after that, Watson took Chicken Shit Bingo on the road and he hasn't stopped since. Over two decades after its start, patrons still line up every Sunday at 4pm to buy $2 tickets and try their luck at a cash prize. During the pandemic, The Little Longhorn Saloon even live streamed chicken shit bingo, and raised money through GoFund-Me to keep the bar open.

These days, everything's back to business as usual, with few changes. The wall behind the stage is still a patchwork of framed photos of musicians who have played there through the years. The rest of the place is still plastered with vintage show flyers and beer signs (including across the ceiling). But the bar now serves craft beer on draught, in addition to over a dozen bottled options, plus wine— and there's even an entire mini-fridge of malt-based Fireball bottles behind the bar. There's also now a point of sale system, so guests aren't required to pay in cash. Just above it you'll see a hand-written sign stating, "Ginny Says: No Fussin', No Cussin', No Hasselin', No Wresslin'." Same rules still apply.

More Locally Loved North Austin Bars:

THE HIDEOUT PUB
12164 TX-1 Loop, Austin, TX 78758

SEOULJU
9515 N Lamar Boulevard #230, Austin, TX 78753

THE BON AIRE
9070 Research Boulevard, Austin, TX 78758

NOSH AND BEVVY
8440 Burnet Road #100, Austin, TX 78757

NIGHT OWL
8315 Burnet Road, Austin, TX 78757

THE VIOLET CROWN
7100 Woodrow Avenue, Austin, TX 78757

BILLY'S ON BURNET
2105 Hancock Drive, Austin, TX 78756

LONG PLAY LOUNGE
704 W St Johns Avenue, Austin, TX 78752

Locally Loved North Austin Breweries And Cideries:

AUSTIN BEERWORKS
3001 Industrial Terrace, Austin, TX 78758

CELIS BREWERY
10001 Metric Boulevard, Austin, TX 78758

HOPSQUAD BREWING CO.
2307 Kramer Lane, Austin, TX 78758

CIRCLE BREWING COMPANY
2340 W Braker Lane b, Austin, TX 78758

FAIRWEATHER CIDER CO.
10609 Metric Boulevard #108, Austin, TX 78758

BLACK STAR CO-OP PUB & BREWERY
7020 Easy Wind Drive #100, Austin, TX 78752

REVELRY KITCHEN + BAR
1410 E 6th Street, Austin, TX 78702

THE BREWTORIUM
6015 Dillard Circle A, Austin, TX 78752

Locally Loved North Austin Dive Bars:

TWIN CREEKS HALL
13400 FM2769, Austin, TX 78726

THE MILL
9112 Anderson Mill Road suite b 100, Austin, TX 78729

THE LOCAL OUTPOST
13201 Pond Springs Road, Austin, TX 78729

THE WATER TANK
7309 McNeil Drive, Austin, TX 78729

RAGGEDY ANNE'S
2113 Wells Branch Parkway #600, Austin, TX 78728

CORONADO HILLS, WINDSOR PARK, AND MUELLER

The Mueller district, located on the former site of the Robert Mueller Municipal Airport, feels like a suburban enclave, but it's located right in the center of town, making it extremely popular with young families. The community, which is northeast of Hyde Park and the University of Texas, features homes and condos of varying sizes and layouts, plus proximity to Mueller Lake Park, community pools, playgrounds, and a children's museum. There's also a grocery store, children's hospital, emergency medical clinic, movie theater, and a handful of restaurants and bars—L'Oca D'Oro, Colleen's Kitchen, B.D. Riley's, and Veracruz Fonda and Bar, to name a few. As Mueller has become more populated and expensive over the years, that same demographic of young families and first-time homeowners has been looking to Windsor Park, a residential neighborhood spanning from East 51st Street to 290 North, between I-35 and Manor Road. Windsor Park is located close enough to Mueller to enjoy all its amenities, and it has a few of its own: Mum Foods, Hank's, and Little Deli & Pizzeria are three popular neighborhood restaurants. However, at the rate this neighborhood is growing in popularity, there seems to be room for much more. Now, Coronado Hills has joined the conversation. The triangular neighborhood, just east of St. John's and nestled between Highways 183, 290, and Cameron Road, offers even more affordable housing as prices rise in Windsor Park.

THE SILVER MEDAL

7100 E Highway 290
Austin, TX 78723

As the old adage goes: if you want something done, you've got to do it yourself. That's exactly why Aaron Bush opened Silver Medal. After two decades of bartending left him feeling burnt out, Bush left the industry. He was working as a mechanic in Windsor Park when he realized that the growing neighborhood could really use a bar, so he started looking around for a spot to open his own place. But with all the surrounding property being snatched up at an alarming rate, he set his sights on a spot just across 290, in the Coronado Hills neighborhood once known as "The Devil's Triangle" because of its seedy reputation.

The building in question was originally a coffee shop for Patton Motor Courts when the airport motel opened in 1953, and then it housed a couple different taquerias over the years. When Bush called the owner of El Charrito to inquire about the property, it just so happened the family was about to list it.

"It was a cool-ass building so I didn't do anything outside, just kinda sealed the place up and tried to make it look like I'd imagined it looked originally," remembers Bush, who opened Silver Medal the day after Thanksgiving 2019. The bar's back patio is scattered with tables and chairs with umbrella coverage, and the El

Charrito sign lives on the back of the building, in honor of its past life. Now, a board in the front beckons: "The Silver Medal: Where Everyone's Almost a Winner." The bar is still flanked by Patton Courts to its left, where rooms are rented by the hour or day. "We don't really get any crossover business," says Bush. "Let's just say the people who go to that motel are...trying to keep a low profile."

The interior, like the exterior, features two-tone, brown and beige walls plus a wood-paneled bar that gives the place a warm 1970s cabin feel. The space is just big enough for a row of bar stools and a handful of mismatched tables. The vintage bar decor came from Bush's own collection: a Yuengling clock, a PBR light-box, a Lone Star shadowbox housing a Colt 45 replica, a poster from a Mastodon show at the original Emo's, and a poster for Hooper, a stuntman movie starring Burt Reynolds. The main pops of color come from a stained glass window, spelling out Silver Medal, which Bush commissioned for the space.

A TV in the bar's corner, next to a vintage cigarette machine, is usually showing a cult classic on VHS or DVD—on my first visit, "Damn It Feels Good to Be a Gangster" was playing over Apocalypse Now—but they'll also take requests and stream movies too. And depending on who's behind the bar, the soundtrack could span from country to punk to psych rock to doom metal.

"When we first opened and people started calling us a dive bar, I was like, 'Man, we're fucking new!' I don't picture a new bar being a dive bar, you know?" laughs Bush. "But I guess a dive is just a comfortable, uncurated bar? At this point, it's not for me to say. If everyone calls us a dive bar, I guess that's what we are."

In true dive bar spirit, the bar program keeps things simple and, most importantly, cheap. During happy hour, which is every day until 7pm, wells are just $3, and $2 Jello shots are always stacked up in the fridge. Budweiser and Lone Star are on tap next to Twisted Tea, which gets mixed with Deep Eddy Lemon to create a John Daly, a boozy version of an Arnold Palmer. And that's the closest to a "house cocktail" that you'll see here. Silver Medal is more of a shot-and-a-beer type place. Malört happens to be such a popular order, there's a sign advertising $6 shots of the infamous spirit—"$10 if you're gonna talk about it."

The tiny space also came with a kitchen no bigger than a food truck, so Bush developed a menu based on a now-shuttered hot dog joint in his hometown of Tyler, Texas. The chili dog is the star of the show—"The chili recipe is a secret," one of the cooks confides in me. "I work here and I don't even know what's in it!"—and Silver Medal punch cards promise your tenth dog for free. There's also a handful of other dogs, a variety of smash burgers with different toppings, plus Frito pie, a BLT, grilled cheese, and even a couple of options for salad, if you're feeling healthy.

It was the bar's food component that ended up being a saving grace when the city went into pandemic lockdown just three months after they opened. Since they are technically a restaurant, they were able to stay open, and became an instantly popular spot for service and music industry friends. Guitarists from Holy Wave and The Sword both work here, and Bush has cast a wide net of bar industry friends in his years working at Emo's, Liberty, and White Horse. Now it has become a popular neighborhood watering hole, attracting a wildly diverse crowd.

"This weekend, we had a fucking bachelorette party in here at the same time as a bunch of fashion punk idiots," describes Bush. "Like it should be, it's a mix of neighborhood folks and friends of the bar."

JOHN DALY

If you enjoy an Arnold Palmer on a hot day, you'll love this boozy version, named after the notoriously boozy golfer John Daly. Silver Medal uses a simple combination of Deep Eddy Lemon vodka and Twisted Tea, but you could alternatively use regular vodka with lemonade or lemon juice.

2 oz. Deep Eddy Lemon Vodka

16-20 oz. Twisted Tea or another boozy tea

Lemon wedge, to garnish

1. Fill a 32 oz. mini pitcher with ice, add the vodka, and fill with your favorite boozy tea.
2. Garnish with the lemon wedge.

CAROUSEL LOUNGE

1110 E 52nd Street
Austin, TX 78723

If you weren't looking for Carousel Lounge, you might not ever turn onto East 52nd Street and find it. And that would be a damn shame, because this historic family-run bar must be preserved at all costs. Tucked on a side street off a strip of Cameron Road filled with fast food and pawn shops, Carousel Lounge sits on the edge of the growing Windsor Park neighborhood, just a stone's throw from the popular Mueller district. But when Myrtle and Cecil Meier opened the club in 1963, it was on the outskirts of town, right by the now-defunct Mueller Airport.

"They loved dancing, drinking, and being around like-minded people," says their daughter Nicki Mebane, who inherited the bar when Cecil passed away in 1988. "[They] got a pretty much loyal clientele from the beginning when the Windsor neighborhood was fairly new."

Over the last 60 years, little has changed at the circus-themed bar. The building's entire facade is painted with vignettes of circus tents, animals, and performers. A sculptural caged giraffe greets those who enter and an antique carousel sits behind the bar. A blue and white striped wall behind the bar contrasts the red padded arm rails and bar stools. A row of bright red booths lines a wall painted with an elephant mural, each table with its own tabletop jukebox. The main room opens up into an even larger second room, where all the walls are covered in murals depicting acrobats, clowns, tight-rope-walking monkeys and, of course, carousel animals. The whole colorful, campy scene looks like a set from a David Lynch movie.

The Meiers never pursued a liquor license, and instead allowed patrons to bring in their own and buy set-ups from the bar. And so, it remains one of the only places in town where you can BYO-liquor. There are many more options for beer, as well as cider and hard seltzer, and most hover around the $3 mark, dropping to $2 at happy hour. And if you must have wine, there's a box of Franzia behind the bar with your name on it.

"It was always very much a Cheers bar, especially in the afternoon after work," says Mebane. "We have always

prided ourselves with knowing your name and having your beer on the bar before you sit down."

The Carousel Lounge was originally open seven days a week, starting at 10 a.m., and featured nightly music from a variety of different bands. Then a blind musician named Jay Clark and his Big Band-inspired backup players The Velvetones became the house band, drawing a crowd for nightly shows. In the 1970s, Clark became a one-man band, playing the saxophone and clarinet while accompanied by a four-track tape recorder. By the 1980s, many of the bar's regular patrons were getting too old to visit. But after Mebane took over operation, she hired a couple college bartenders, including her son, who worked there part-time while going to Texas State. Suddenly, the place was revived with a young audience who was intrigued by the bar's retro, zany appeal, and Carousel became known for its very mixed demographic of old timers, punk rockers and undergrads.

After 30 years of entertaining at the Carousel Lounge, Clark retired in the late 1990s, and the bar continued to serve as a stage—often for arty, experimental, genre-defying acts that play on the ground level—there's no actual elevated stage—in front of a giant pink elephant. There's music every night they're open, with belly dancers performing once a month and several regular bands that play monthly.

A testament to this time capsule of a bar, the same telephone booth has been tucked in the corner since 1963. Though the telephone inside is still operational, it serves more as a photo prop than anything these days. "I just wanted to keep [the bar] as original as possible," says Mebane. And we sure are glad she did.

More Locally Loved Coronado Hills, Windsor Park, and Mueller Bars:

KNOMAD BAR
1213 Corona Drive, Austin, TX 78723

HANK'S
5811 Berkman Drive, Austin, TX 78723

B.D. RILEY'S
1905 Aldrich Street #130, Austin, TX 78723

HALCYON
1905 Aldrich Street suite 110 suite 110, Austin, TX 78723

WHICHCRAFT TAP ROOM & BOTTLE SHOP
1900 Simond Avenue #200, Austin, TX 78723

NORTH LOOP

Austin's North Loop neighborhood, located just northeast of the University of Texas campus, is a tree-lined community filled with single-family homes erected after World War II. The neighborhood is dissected by North Loop Boulevard, a quirky and walkable street filled with vintage shops like Room Service Vintage and other indie stores, such as Breakaway Records, Forbidden Fruit, and Monkeywrench Books, plus restaurants like Home Slice and Foreign & Domestic and several great bars. "North Loop is one of the last vestiges of old Austin," says Jessica Sanders, owner of DrinkWell (page 43). "There's enough character on this street for people to have a culturally rich experience that still feels authentic." You could easily spend the day in this neighborhood, wandering from shop to shop, with delicious food and drink sprinkled throughout.

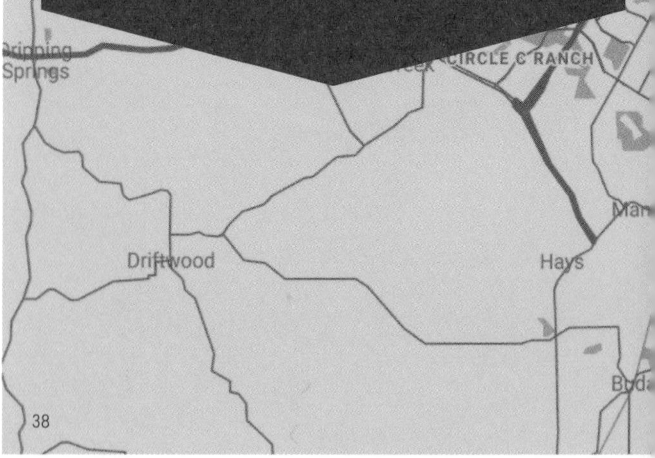

Dripping Springs

CIRCLE C RANCH

Driftwood

Hays

BARFLY'S

5420-B, 5420 Airport Boulevard
Austin, TX 78751

When I discovered Barfly's in my early Austin years, it felt like I'd found a speakeasy long before such clandestine bars were trendy. That's mainly because it was tucked away above a burger joint, and accessible by a green awning-shaded staircase along the side of the building. But don't expect to find any mixologists in suspenders up those stairs. What you will find is a dark, cool respite from the Texas heat—no windows here—a familiar bar staf, and stiff pours for miraculous prices.

Erected in 1960, the building originally housed a restaurant called Buckboard. Worn wooden floors and exposed ceiling beams showcase the simple beauty of the structure, and the bricks used in the space were taken from an old, dismantled train depot. The walls are covered with framed vintage Guinness posters and various keepsakes, drawings, and stickers added by regulars through the years. A collection of sunglasses and keys dangle above the bar, in a makeshift, accidentally decorative lost-and-found. And the jukebox is always cranked up to do justice to rowdy greats like Queens of the Stone Age, The Misfits, Murder City Devils, At the Drive-In, AC/DC, and Parquet Courts.

After bartending and managing bars and clubs for close to a decade, Marcos Canchola says, "I decided that I had fallen off enough barstools that I should open my own." He and a high school classmate, the late Keith Young, scraped their money together and opened Barfly's in 2001, on Pi Day, March 14. "Growing up in El Paso, we would cross the border to Juárez," remembers Canchola. "Barfly's has pieces of Kentucky Club, Sarawak's, Tequila Derby, Superior, and Fred's, where we cut our teeth."

After seeing immediate success with Barfly's, the two partnered with Brian Hyde to open MugShots the very next year, and the beloved downtown dive bar thrived on East 7th Street until it sadly shuttered in 2020 after being shut down during the pandemic. Canchola and Hyde also co-own and operate The Hideout Pub, Bender, Violet Crown Social Club, and Pour House Pints & Pies. At press time, Canchola was working on permitting for the space below Barfly's, which will become a bar and grill named The Golden Hour, after the bar in the movie *Barfly*.

While Canchola keeps drinks reasonably priced at all the bars mentioned above, Barfly's is known for its particularly stiff, cheap pours. Ask if there's specials and they'll tell you "everything's special"—and it's true. Wells are $4 and premium drinks just $6, in a city where it's increasingly hard to find single call drinks priced in the single digits. A Lone Star and shot of Jameson is the regulars' drink of choice. As their website states, "Our drinks are cheap so you don't have to be"—in other words, tip your bartender well!

If the drinks, music and company aren't enough to hold your attention, there's also a good amount of entertainment packed inside the bar, from foosball to Silver Strike Bowling to old school arcade games like Ms. Pacman and Galaga. They've also managed to fit three pool tables into the galley of a space. I once watched someone do the worm on top of one during a dance-off gone wild.

On any given night, there's a few regulars posted up at the bar, with their attention turned to whatever movie is playing on the screen behind it, accompanied by the punk- and metal-dominant soundtrack. A red staircase on the back of the building leads to a patio where smokers will spend their entire night, only coming inside long enough to replenish their drinks... and maybe feed the jukebox a little more.

DRINKWELL

207 E 53rd Street
Austin, TX 78751

Jessica Sanders set out to make the sort of bar she wished existed. She was living in New York when the craft cocktail Renaissance began in the aughts, and found herself inspired by bars like Death & Co and PDT. "I was blown away in terms of the artistry behind it, and the idea that you could do what you do with food, but with liquor, was really compelling to me," Sanders remembers. "But the pretentiousness of cocktail bars hadn't been peeled away yet because everything was about the product and nothing was about the people. DrinkWell was born to marry these things—to take the familiarity and warmth of a neighborhood bar but present a quality product."

There was just one small detail: Sanders' hospitality experience was limited to a stint at Starbucks in college. So she taught herself everything she could about wine, spirits, and cocktails through independent study and classes. She left her corporate job as a marketer for *Forbes* magazine and moved to Austin with the intent of opening a bar. "I always tell people DrinkWell should have never been a success because the first bar I tended was my own," says Sanders with a laugh.

When she got to town, she visited the few cocktail bars that existed in Austin at the time. One was Tigress Pub (page 51), where she was incredibly inspired by proprietor Pam Pritchard, who had also left an entirely

different industry to open her bar. She also fell in love with North Loop Boulevard, where there just happened to be another space available.

The 1960 building had served as many things in its lifetime: among them a vintage clothing store, a skateboard shop, a massage parlor, and a hair salon. But it had never been a food or beverage operation so all the plumbing needed to be redone. Sanders recalls trying to take on as many tasks as she could to save money, including her first try at demolition. After she returned from Home Depot with a comically small mallet— and proceeded to use it to knock down walls— her contractor framed it, and it still hangs at the entrance of the bar.

Sanders says she was inspired by a number of bars when designing the space and program: namely Cure in Nola, Anvil in Houston, and Teardrop Lounge in Portland. "They're the kind of bars where you don't need a special occasion to go there," she describes. "They feel comfortable and familiar, but you also know that the product being put out is really intentional, the food and drinks are really well-cared for, and the people are well-cared for too."

When DrinkWell opened in February 2012, it was immediately embraced by the neighborhood. The small space is bathed in neutral tones and flooded with sunlight, a stark contrast to many of the dark and brooding cocktail bars of that era. Shiplap, brick, concrete, and leather provide contrasting tactile textures lit by elegant pendant lights. The size of the space actually makes it feel more inviting, and 36 seats fit inside without feeling crowded whatsoever. The simple, but warm, design really allows the food and drink to shine. Yes, there's even a tiny kitchen where her team creates fantastic bar food, from weekend special spicy Thai jam mussels and fries to a Wagyu burger that's been called one of the best in town.

The bar is stocked with over 100 different whiskies and 30 different gins, and the cocktails served here are consistently some of the best in town. Each house cocktail is perfectly balanced and refined, often incorporating culinary techniques and components like tomato-fig jam, garam masala, radish, or lime leaf oil, and made complex with the addition of aperitifs, vermouths, sherries, and liqueurs. A list of classic cocktails is also always available and the gimlet, made exceptional with a house-made lime cordial, remains one of the most popular orders.

Coming full circle, Sanders now finds herself leading cocktail classes like the ones that helped expand her knowledge and usher her into the industry. Libation Bible School, which has been occurring once a month for the last seven years, helps her students develop a vocabulary around spirits. She's currently planning a pro-am cocktail competition where the winner will get to add a drink of their creation to DrinkWell's cocktail menu.

During COVID, the bar never closed. Instead, Sanders picked up consulting work and maintained a robust to-go program to keep everyone employed. "I was the Chief Executive Delivery Driver for 9 months," she recalls. She also expanded the patio, adding 24 more seats to the bar so they could accommodate even more guests. When they were able to reopen for dine-in customers in May 2020, Sanders was inspired by other local restaurants—especially L'Oca d'Oro—and worked with her accountant to revamp the pay structure. Now no one on the staff makes less than $16 an hour base pay, and all guest checks include a 20% Employee Wellness Charge that goes toward those wages and as well as medical insurance and subsidized mental healthcare for all employees.

With stronger revenue than ever and zero turnover in the last three years, Sanders may have found the magic formula. When DrinkWell turned ten years old in 2022, they won Cocktail Bar of the Year at the National Bar & Restaurant Expo and made the top ten list of Best U.S. Cocktail Bars for Tales of the Cocktail's Spirited Awards. While Sanders was thrilled with these milestone achievements, she gets just as excited when she talks about the team's commitment to philanthropy.

"The entire staff, individually and collectively, is very community-minded," she says. "The work that we do in the business is not limited to these four walls." They host Barman's Fund events to support local nonprofits like Casa Marianella, a shelter for women and children escaping violence. And two years ago they launched

House of Effervescence, a program celebrating champagne, sparkling wine, drag culture, and queer culture.
All proceeds from those events go to allgo, a queer-fo-
cused charity that supports people of color with health
and wellness programs.

This is all to say that DrinkWell is doing much more than
just keeping the community well-fed and hydrated,
which makes them the best kind of neighborhood bar.

WORKHORSE BAR

100 North Loop Boulevard E, Suite B
Austin, TX 78751

Workhorse is the kind of bar you stop in for "one drink," but it's several hours later before you end up teetering back out into the world. It happens to the best of us, and owner Brent Boyles has witnessed it too many times to count. "It all starts with the bartender, who has probably been here for four to five years, so you feel like you know someone," he describes. "Then someone walks in the door who you met last week, then your good friend who you didn't know came here walks in, and so on and so forth. The next thing you know, you stayed up late hanging with friends on a Tuesday."

It's no surprise the bar feels as comfy as hanging out at a friend's house, because that's where the idea for Workhorse all started. Boyles worked at a number of Austin bars and restaurants while studying at the University of Texas. When he moved in with his college friend Steve Ettle, they turned their garage into a game room with a kegerator and a 200-disc CD change. Wheels began to turn as he toyed with the idea of opening a bar someday. A couple years after graduation, Boyles was still working in the service industry and Ettle asked if he was serious about that bar idea. The two put their heads together, figured out a financing plan and began to design their first bar, which opened in April 2012. Though Ettle sold his half of Workhorse to Boyles

a couple of years ago, the two are still partners in another bar, Back Lot, which they own with a third partner.

This North Loop retail space was built in the 1950s, most likely as an auto garage to start, though it's also been a dry cleaners, a taqueria and a punk rock pizza joint called The Parlor (among other things). The dark wood paneling running around the bottom half of the wall matches the tables, chairs and table caddies they crafted by hand before opening. The cream wall is hung with black and white photos of various Austin landmarks under construction, which Boyles says was inspired by "the significance of this being our first place and that every place, even the Capitol, started somewhere. [We] just liked the idea of capturing parts of Austin before they became what we know them as today."

They also had friends paint the big acrylic-on-canvas replicas of album covers: The Beatles' Revolver, Queen's Night at the Opera, Stone Temple Pilots' Purple, and

The Band's Music From Big Pink. The great white whale overturning a ship is the album cover from Mastodon's Leviathan album, and Boyles painted that one himself. They were actually considering several different songs by the influential metal band when naming the bar, but settled on Workhorse because it's "not pretentious, and representative of all the hardworking individuals in this neighborhood," explains Boyle. "Clearly we liked Mastodon a lot when we opened and still do."

Out on the back patio, there's a map of Texas breweries Boyle also painted, although he points out it was immediately outdated due to all the breweries that opened. The log stools they originally made for inside the bar now live outside, and a wall of beer signs honors some of their favorites. Behind the bar, there are always around fifty beers on tap, including favorites like St. Elmo Carl Kölsch, Pinthouse Electric Jellyfish and Bell's Two Hearted Ale. Ten of those are rotating seasonal picks, and there's always a selection of $3 drafts. Though Workhorse is known as a beer destination, they also offer a short list of cocktails, and the $6 Workhorse Margarita, made with Paula's Texas Orange and fresh lime juice, is not to be missed.

"We never wanted to be beer snobs or make craft cocktails," says Boyles. "When we first opened there were some bars with staff that looked down their nose at you if you ordered a Lone Star, or didn't know what kind of bourbon you wanted. We have good beers and some tasty cocktails, but the staff's goal is to help you find what makes you happy."

From the bar, you can see right into the small, open-air kitchen where they make solid burgers, fulfilling salads and snacks like fried pickles, white wings, and Parmesan fries. It would take some sort of special willpower to resist ordering something after you've had a couple drinks and the intoxicating smell of grilled onions wafts out of there. And this, my friends, is how you never leave Workhorse.

THE TIGRESS PUB

100 West N Loop Boulevard, Unit G
Austin, TX 78751

I'll set the scene for you: it was December, and I was looking for the perfect place for a first date. Work schedules and COVID scares had kept us from meeting for over a month, so the setting for our first face-to-face felt even more significant. It had to be comfortable and laid back—somewhere we could settle in and converse with few distractions. Ideally, a place with high quality, but unpretentious, drinks. When he said he was craving a hot cocktail, I knew just the place: The Tigress Pub, which always serves hot toddies and Irish coffee on cool nights.

This unassuming little cocktail bar fits in perfectly on North Loop Boulevard with its post-punk, DIY aesthetic. It's set in a 1960s retail space that used to house Asahi Imports Japanese market, with faux-finished red and turquoise walls, coppery ceiling tiles, and a concrete floor still griddled from the tiles laid upon it in a past life. High-back wooden benches and little stained-glass panels hanging in the front windows hint at the bar's British pub inspiration, and a small back patio is scattered with little turquoise tables and mismatched folding chairs. The tiny little L-shaped bar fits no more than five bar stools and appears, at first glance, to have a pretty modest collection of spirits. But make no mistake: Tigress takes its craft cocktails seriously, and keeps them reasonably priced to boot.

Owner Pam Pritchard took the path less traveled to becoming a bar owner. Her B.S. in Microbiology led her to work in hospital labs for years until she knew it was time for a change, and decided that she wanted to own her

own business. "The bar business came about because of a few things," recalls Pritchard matter-of-factly. "I like people, I like tasting, I enjoy mixing things up and cooking, and I don't have a problem with alcohol. The bar business seemed to be a good fit for me."

At the time, Pritchard lived in Santa Barbara but after several visits to the Live Music Capital, she knew Austin was the place for her bar concept. She dedicated six serious years of research toward her goal, studying cocktails, interviewing bar owners and taking notes on what she liked about other bars. After six more months of seeking out her location, she opened Tigress Pub in May 2010.

"I wanted a neighborhood bar that just happened to serve up excellent cocktails, so the bar was designed to be friendly and welcoming," says Pritchard, who describes Tigress as her own idea of a British pub. "The Tigress name comes from seeing the English style of naming pubs which often comes with a picture of that thing. For example, The Queen's Head, The Flower Pot, Five Lamps, The Dolphin. I have a little ceramic tiger collection at home, and so a friend suggested I name it The Tigress."

At this pub, the focus isn't on beer, though they do serve 20-ounce "proper pints" of rotating local brew on tap. What Tigress is best known for, however, is their well-made classics—most under $10—as well as a list of signature cocktails that changes about every six weeks. The menu also features a short list of low-ABV and non-alcoholic cocktails, in an effort to offer something for everyone.

The pub, which opens every day of the week at 4pm and 3pm on weekends, has a solid following of regulars and a robust event calendar. Nola Mondays feature a New Orleans-themed cocktail menu, tarot readings, and a jazz soundtrack. Tropical Tuesdays bring all-night tiki drink specials, and Hawaiian shirts are encouraged. Wednesday is happy hour all day, and Signature Saturdays mean $2 off all the signature cocktails until 8pm. In addition to that, they're constantly hosting one-off events, from food pop-ups and vintage markets to Horror Tiki night, BYO-vinyl nights and birthday parties for greats like Selena and Dolly Parton.

"As my mentor told me, 'It's your bar, make it the way you like it,'" says Pritchard. "'Folks that like what you like will enjoy it and bring their friends and everyone will get along great.' And that is exactly what has happened."

THE GREEN DRINK

Pritchard developed The Green Drink as a seasonal special based on a cocktail called The Shrinebuilder, created at The Whistler in Chicago. The original is a swizzle cocktail that comes over fine crushed ice, but this version is shaken and served up in a cocktail glass. "We just have it for the months of March and October because, with South by Southwest and football season, the bar would slow down and this has always been a good way to keep afloat during those months. Now the bar is coming on 13 years in May and those are now our busiest months!" Coincidence? You be the judge.

1 ½ oz. green Chartreuse

1 oz. Verdita

¾ oz. Velvet Falernum

½ oz. fresh lime juice

1. Add all of the ingredients to a cocktail shaker, add ice, and shake vigorously.

2. Double strain into a chilled martini glass, then smack and add mint leaf to the top for garnish.

Verdita: Blend equal parts lime juice and fresh pineapple chunks into a food processor, then add ½ seeded jalapeño and equal parts fresh cilantro and mint. Filter the juice through a nut bag to remove all the fiber parts before using.

More Locally Loved North Loop and Highland Bars:

EASY TIGER AT THE LINC
6406 N Interstate 35 Frontage Road, Suite 1100, Austin, TX 78752

SPOKESMAN HIGHLAND
6015 Dillard Circle #B, Austin, TX 78752

LAZARUS BREWING CO.
803 Airport Boulevard, Austin, TX 78751

THE GRAND
4631 Airport Boulevard, Austin, TX 78751

ROSEDALE, HYDE PARK, NORTH UNIVERSITY, AND UT CAMPUS

The University of Texas campus is located about a mile north of the Texas State Capitol, distinguishable in the skyline by the UT Tower. Just south of campus, you'll find the oldest beer garden in the U.S., Scholz Garten (page 68), where students, professors, politicians, and football fans congregate over cold pints. Guadalupe Street borders the campus on the west, and it is referred to as "the Drag" from Martin Luther King Boulevard to 29th Street. This area of town was once home to independent businesses that defined the early days of Austin—from the legendary Chicano-turned-punk club Raul's and the equally legendary venue Rome Inn to beloved bohemian French café Les Amis and Inner Sanctum Records, the first indie record shop in Texas. But as rents began to rise, the entire strip changed in the 1990s and early aughts. The Drag is now filled with corporate retail shops, coffee shops, and fast-casual eateries, but places like Hole in the Wall (page 64) and the historic burger joint Dirty Martin's Place

Spr

Driftwood

Hays

are still holding on strong. On the north edge of campus, you'll find Crown & Anchor and Posse East, two long-standing and well-loved sports bars, as well as Tweedy's Bar, a revival of Spider House, a 24-hour coffeehouse and bar that was an Austin institution from 1995 to 2020.

Hyde Park is a charming area located north of campus, just west of I-35 between 38th and 51st Street. Wide, shady streets are lined with Victorian and Craftsman houses, with some duplexes and small apartment complexes peppered in too. Though most of Hyde Park is residential, there is a strip of cafés and shops along its eastern and western perimeters, with longstanding favorites like Quack's 43rd Street Bakery and Julio's Café, plus newer additions like Mongers, Antonelli's Cheese Shop, and Uncle Nicky's. Just northwest of campus is Rosedale, another cute residential, leaf-shaded neighborhood filled with bungalows from the 1930s and 1940s. It is here that Medical Parkway turns into the southern end of Burnet Road, which is filled with restaurants, food trucks, and shops as it makes its way toward Brentwood and Allandale.

DRAUGHT HOUSE

4112 Medical Parkway
Austin, TX 78756

The Draught House could very well be a half-timbered house in the Bavarian countryside— but instead it is tucked between doctor's offices on Medical Parkway. If it looks similar to another Austin bar, that's because it is. Wayne and Gay Overton managed The Tavern (page 172), then gave up a short-lived foray into farming to build The Draught House in the same style as its North Lamar inspiration. They also dug a cellar to house the kegs for the 18 draught lines that were originally in place, and constructed the bar, and all the tables and chairs, by hand. The Draught House opened in June 1969 and the Overtons ran it successfully for the next 25 years.

When the lease on the Draught House became available in 1995, Josh Wilson and some partners reopened it; today, Wilson and his wife Debbie are the owners. A 7-barrel brewing system was added and the number of beer taps was increased to 74, with 20 of those pouring house brews. Wilson, who got his start brewing at the Bitter End, a now-closed Austin brewpub, while going to film school at UT, brews around 700 barrels a year. All his beer is unfiltered, and no clarifying agents are used.

"Currently I am producing mostly American and English styles with an emphasis on hops," says Wilson. "We always have three cask and three nitro beers, at least three IPAs, and some sour and dark beers on tap as well. Additionally, there will always be some seasonal beers, such as Lime Bomb in the warmer months."

Little has changed about the interior over the years, and that is intentional. Wilson and his partners simply wanted to maintain and honor the Overtons' original vision for the space they poured so much into. The original handmade furniture, which has been carved with initials through the years, has a lot to do with the pub's charm.

"Apparently more people carried knives back then and customers immediately began to chisel out the tables," says Wilson. "The story is that [Wayne Overton] was not happy about this but was not successful in stopping it. I had the tables rebuilt and refinished a few years ago, taking care to preserve the carvings, and they are now a nice piece of history. People will occasionally come in and see their handiwork from years ago."

Stained glass steins in the double swinging doors at the entrance still welcome each guest. The walls are hung with a few vintage British pub signs, plus shelves of relics like old bottles, wooden beer crates and barrel signs. Of course, a few screens have been added, both for games and for displaying the current beer offerings. And though an Ice Cold Beer retro arcade game has appeared, darts remain the entertainment of choice; the dartboards in the corner of the pub have to be two of the most frequently used in town. From 1995 to 2012, there was a dentist's office on the second floor of the building, and patients used to get tokens to come down and get a beer afterward. Wilson is currently working on renovating the space into a second level for the bar.

Historically, the Draught House parking lot would turn into a literal tailgating party, with regulars bringing folding chairs and sitting on the back of their trucks with pitchers of beer. These days, a red and white striped tent protects rows of benches in the beer garden and strands of lights twinkle overhead. Some years ago, Wilson replaced the rotation of different food trucks with one owned by the bar. Little House serves fish and chips, of course, with hand cut Belgian fries—as well as a solid menu of burgers, fried brussels sprouts, falafel and hummus, and more.

Each year, the Draught House throws a massive anniversary shindig with special tappings of cellars and barrel-aged brews, live music, DJs, commemorative glasses, and other schwag. "We have families from the neighborhood, urban professionals, students, craft beer fans of all ages," says Wilson, "It is not uncommon for parents who frequented the Draught House in college to come back with their kids, who are now UT students. I think the combination of warm atmosphere, friendly crowds, and great beer keeps the locals coming back."

HOPFIELDS

3110 Guadalupe Street, #400
Austin, TX 78705

On the outside, Hopfields looks like an unassuming storefront in a strip of businesses on the Drag. But step inside and you've entered a rustic, charming little gastropub that feels like it could be located in a small French hamlet.

When Bay Anthon and Lindsay Anthon-Zuloaga opened the little bar in 2011, they shared a wall with a yoga studio. The structure, which was originally built in the 1950s, was the site of the city's first Half Price Books, and a scene from the iconic Austin movie Slackers had been filmed there. They painted the brick facade green, bathed the exposed brick inside in white, and filled the rest of the space with dark wooden picnic tables, bistro tables, and chairs. Reclaimed church pew benches line the perimeter of the dining space and the bar is built from a patchwork of wood pieces. As you walk further back, you'll find romantic little candlelit nooks leading out to a spacious, tree-shaded patio.

A 40-tap wall boasts their constantly changing, well-curated selection of beer from around the world—and, refreshingly, it spans beyond the offerings you'll see repeated at so many other bars. However, you will often see the freshest pours from favorites like Jester King Brewery, Fair State Brewing Cooperative, Duvel Moortgat Brewery, Unibroue, Odell Brewing Company, and Dutchess Ales, among others. They also feature a selection of aged and cellared beer selections, a

French-leaning wine list and, since getting their full liquor license during the pandemic, they now offer a menu of classic cocktails and riffs on classics. While Hopfields is much more than a beer bar, the concept started with Anthon's love of craft brew.

"I started in tech and the running joke was drinking craft beer was like golf of the tech world," he remembers. "Instead of hitting the links, we would talk shop over craft beers. I just became a fanatic and did as much travel and research as possible to become more acquainted with craft beer."

While the founding duo is no longer together—Anthon is now the sole operator—Anthon-Zuloaga's French background is what inspired the menu, and her mother helped create many of the original recipes. Right out of the gate, the gastropub became known for its French onion soup, steak frites and the decadent Pascal burger, draped with silky caramelized onions and melty Camembert, with cornichons and grain mustard lending acidity and punch. However, the kitchen has

also evolved and become refined through the years, adding items like bouillabaisse and escargot dumplings with miso butter, plus nightly specials featuring local, seasonal ingredients.

And best of all, the kitchen is open each night until midnight, which is surprisingly rare, even this close to UT's campus. They also serve a brunch menu on both Saturdays and Sundays, and host plenty of one-off events, from World Cup and Austin FC watch parties to crawfish boils and pint nights.

"We try to be the best without taking ourselves too seriously," says Anthon. "It is about the human experience of enjoying each other over the best food and drink we can create. So, in a nutshell, it's about people having warm feelings and full bellies."

FRENCH 77

A French 77 is a spin on the more commonly known French 75, made by substituting elderflower liqueur for simple syrup. While the original was created in 1915 at Harry's Bar in Paris, the spin-off was made by Simon Difford as recently as 2006. This is a popular drink at Hopfields' New Year's Eve parties, but this classy and sneakily high-octane cocktail is great any time of year.

1 oz. Zephyr gin

½ oz. St-Germain

½ oz. fresh lemon juice

2 oz. sparkling wine (Hopfields uses a Crémant de Bourgogne Blanc de Blancs)

Lemon peel twist, to garnish

1. Add gin, St. Germain and lemon juice to a cocktail shaker with ice and shake vigorously until the outside of the tin is icy.

2. Strain into a champagne flute and top off with bubbles before garnishing with lemon peel twist.

HOLE IN THE WALL

2538 Guadalupe Street
Austin, TX 78705

Doug Cugini moved to Austin from Buffalo to help his parents, who ran truck stop diners, open one near campus. In 1974, he scored a handshake deal on the vacant dry cleaners on Guadalupe and 26th Street and named it Hole in the Wall, after the gang from Butch Cassidy and the Sundance Kid. They served chicken fried steak, enchiladas, and sandwiches, with blue plate specials for just $1.29—you can still see the old menus behind a glass case right outside the bathroom. The back room was a game room filled with pool tables, pin-ball machines, foosball, arcade games, and a jukebox.

It was never actually meant to be a music venue—until buskers who normally played on the Drag talked their way into performing right up against the front window, where a Texas flag-draped stage now features more inti-mate acoustic shows. Soon enough, local legends like Doug Sahm, Blaze Foley, and Townes Van Zandt began to make regular appearances. By the 1980s, HITW was known as a certified venue, and went on to become a launching pad for artists like Spoon, Fastball, Gary Clark, Black Joe Lewis, Shakey Graves, and Bob Schnei-der. The number of bands who have played on Hole in the Wall's front and back stages is far too long to list.

Starting in the late 1990s, the bar went through several changes of ownership, and even shut down for a short period of time, but in 2008 it was sold to Will Tanner, a San Antonio native who operated bars and restaurants in El Paso. Tanner, a musician himself, bought the bar because he thought it would be a viable business, but it was only when he started running it that he realized the cultural significance of the second oldest-running venue in the city, after The Broken Spoke (page 284), which opened in 1964.

For every musician that's walked through its doors, there are dozens of stories— and even more rumors— about their goings-on inside. Like the time Stevie Ray Vaughan wailed on the guitar until 3am while his limousine sat outside collecting parking tickets. Or when David Byrne showed up to dance at a disco-themed hoot night. Courtney Love and Dave Grohl have both tagged the bathrooms, and Spoon filmed the video for their song "Jealousy" in there too. And when I say those bathrooms are covered in graffiti... they might just be the most feverishly scribbled-on loos in the city. And the ladies' room, with its side-by-side toilets sans stalls, is simply iconic.

It's hard to miss the bar, with its canary yellow facade and matching marquee announcing the night's performers, always with a few bulbs blown out. And since it's the original marquee, it also says "arcade restaurant," of which it is neither. The Bob Dylan mural on the south-facing wall was painted by prolific local muralist Federico Archuleta, originally to promote a Bob Dylan hoot night. The front door unsurprisingly looks like it has taken a beating over the years, but the arched blue, brown, and white stained-glass window in it has survived, and still spells out "Established 1974." When you pull on the baseball bat handle to enter, the original wooden bar stretches down the length of the first room, punctuated with classic black bar stools, cracked from years of wear. The venue, which was beer-only for years, now serves margaritas and "shitty lemonade," but pitchers of Lone Star, which drop to just $10 during happy hour, are still a more common order.

Right by the photobooth, which is plastered with photostrips and stickers like the rest of the place, a black-and-white collage honors some of HITW's key players through the years. The back bar is home to the main stage, where most shows take place these days, as well as karaoke nights that get pretty rowdy. The alley alongside the building serves as the outdoor patio, which has picnic tables spread out, as well as a pool table set outside a space where East Side Kings ran a ramen shop for a brief period of time.

HITW had to shut down for seven months during pandemic lockdown and, though they have been open and hosting live music every day of the week since reopening, a rumor will still surface every now and then that the bar is in danger of closing. This is all the more reason to sidle up the bar, order a drink, and stay for a show. After all, we can't have Austin without Hole in the Wall.

SCHOLZ GARTEN

1607 San Jacinto Boulevard
Austin, TX 78701

The oldest continuously operating tavern in Texas is located just two blocks south of UT campus, on San Jacinto Boulevard. In 1862, German immigrant August Scholz, a bookbinder by trade, purchased the property at San Jacinto and 17th for $2,400 and operated a boarding house on site. In 1866, he opened a saloon and biergarten, naming it Scholz Garten, and it soon became a popular meeting place for Austin's German population, which was quickly growing in the late 1800s. The important cultural hub started to become known for its entertainment, most notably a summer-long Sunday concert series with a menagerie, fireworks, hot-air balloon rides on 17th Street and performances by the Austin Symphony Orchestra.

After Scholz's death in 1891, the property changed hands several times before a German singing club called The Austin Saengerrunde purchased it in 1908. They erected a spacious hall next door, which is still there and rented for weddings, reunions, and birthdays. And because bowling (kegeln) is a big part of German culture, they also built a bowling alley and started a bowling club. The six-lane alley, which features paper scorecards and antique bowling shoes, is now one of the oldest continuously operating bowling centers in the United States, and it's still only open to members of the Saengerrunde Bowling Club, or available for rental.

Scholz Garten survived Prohibition thanks to the Austin Saengerrunde, who sold nonalcoholic "Bone Dry Beer" on premises and developed the German food program. Though Prohibition ended in 1933, it wasn't until 1937 that they reopened the beer garden to the public. The biergarten changed hands numerous times through the years, but always remained an important part of history. Lady Bird Johnson was a member of the Bored Martyrs Society, a University of Texas women's social club that held monthly meetings at Scholz Garten. The University of Texas football team is said to have celebrated its first undefeated season at the biergarten in 1893, and the bar remains an uber popular spot for Texas Longhorn fans to tailgate during games. Professors and students have frequented the bar since the university's founding, and it's been an important meeting place for politicians as well. The site of numerous political rallies and fund-raisers, Scholz is interestingly a safe zone for all political groups, and it's said that liberal-leaning patrons would meet out in the biergarten while conservatives gathered inside.

"I have a soft space for iconic concepts and there's nothing more iconic than Scholz," says hospitality veteran Dan Smith. "It certainly is a social community center . . . it's a little bit of everything to everybody."

In 2017, a group of investors, led by Smith, took over operations. While there were some improvements and upgrades made to the kitchen, dining room and biergarten, they were done very conscientiously, with respect to the cherished community hub. "We are super careful with everything we do to make sure we preserve the heritage of the space and the character of it," Smith assures. As a result, Scholz Garten's aesthetic hasn't changed much at all. The over 150-year-old bar's interior remains mostly untouched, with its original dark wooden bar, beautiful antique stein in the center of the backbar, dark green ceiling and framed black-and-white photos from Austin in years past. The spacious biergarten's many picnic tables remain shaded by the building's awning, umbrellas, and leafy tree boughs. The outdoor wooden stage, with its mountainous Bavarian backdrop, is again host to live music, from one-off shows to SXSW showcases to KUTX recordings, solidifying Scholz Garten as the entertainment hub it has always been.

Scholz features 28 beers on tap, with a focus on German and European beers poured alongside local craft beers. They also secured a liquor license, so the historically beer-only bar now sells cocktails, with their vodka cherry limeades and Old Fashioneds being the top sellers. The menu was returned to its German roots but given a Texas twist. Guests can build their own sandwich from a variety of sausages like Green Chile and Cheddar, Weisswurst (pork, bacon, lemon, ginger and parsley), and Jackalope (a blend of pork, rabbit and antelope), or enjoy creations like the Piggie Smalls (green chile and cheddar pork sausage topped with spaetzle mac and cheese and peppers and a side of Scholz BBQ sauce). There's also craveable snacks like Reuban waffle fries and sauerkraut potato cheese balls, plus dinner plates like wienerschnitzel and jägerschnitzel, served with red cabbage and house-made spaetzle. On Old World Wednesdays, they feature Texas-made charcuterie boards and a traditional oompah band and, during annual celebrations like Maifest and AustOberfest, the biergarten explodes into a full celebration of German heritage, with live music, polka dancing, and stein-holding competitions.

"Every time I walk into Scholz, I feel blessed to be a part of the history of such a special place," says Smith.

DRINK LIKE A LOCAL AUSTIN

More Locally Loved Rosedale, Hyde Park, and Campus Area Bars:

WINE FOR THE PEOPLE:
1601 W 38th Street, Suite 1, Austin, TX 78731

UNCLE NICKY'S
4222 Duval Street, Austin, TX 78751

BACK LOT
606 Maiden Lane, Austin, TX 78705

HONEY MOON SPIRIT LOUNGE
624 W 34th Street, Austin, TX 78705

TWEEDY'S
2908 Fruth Street, Austin, TX 78705

CROWN & ANCHOR PUB
2911 San Jacinto Boulevard, Austin, TX 78705

POSSE EAST
2900 Duval Street, Austin, TX 78705

DIVE BAR
1703 Guadalupe Street, Austin, TX 78701

MLK, MANOR ROAD, AND AIRPORT BOULEVARD

Martin Luther King Jr. Boulevard, which was 19th Street until the name was changed in the 1970s, connects the west side of the city to the east, and runs along the southern border of UT's campus. The section of the street near campus is filled with hotels and fast-food spots, but once you pass under I-35 and enter East Austin, you'll notice a discernible change as the street becomes a neighborhood. Numbered streets cross with others like Chicon, Poquito, and Chestnut to form a grid peppered with houses. While some original single-family homes have survived, there are increasingly more large, renovated houses and duplexes all throughout the Eastside. Manor Road, which runs parallel to MLK just a few blocks north, features some more affordable apartment complexes, popular with students and recent grads. Both MLK and Manor are now home to coffee shops, like Bennu and Thunderbird, restaurants such as Dai Due, Vic and Al's, and Este, and plenty of bars. While gentrification is largely responsible for this type of growth, places like Sour Duck Market and The Wheel (page 76) strive to maintain accessible prices so they can remain hubs for the community. Both streets cross Airport Boulevard, just south of the Mueller district, which is starting to see some change and will undoubtedly see more in coming years with continued development. While much of Airport Boulevard, south of MLK, is dedicated to fast food, auto sales, and convenience stores, the area between MLK and Manor is now home to several bars that have quickly become staples of the neighborhood, like the family-friendly Batch Craft Beer & Kolaches, and Skylark Lounge (page 83), an homage to the juke joints of Austin past.

THE WHEEL

1902 E Martin Luther King Jr Boulevard B
Austin, TX 78702

If its name is any indication, The Wheel is a biker bar...
but instead of choppers and cruisers lined up out
front, you'll find fixed gears and hybrids locked to the
rack. You see, this watering hole is a celebration of hu-
man-powered machines—and the humans who power
them. And to dispel any confusion, their Instagram profile promises they're "the worst bike shop in Austin."

Blink and you'll miss this tiny bar folded into the corner
of a quad of local businesses on East MLK between
Chicon and Poquito. The Wheel is attached to the Monarch Liquor store, adjacent to Austin Daily Press and
diagonal to Juiceland, with a small lot connecting the
three buildings. That means parking is quite limited,
which is all the more reason to cycle. FBR Management,
the hospitality group known for its preservation of institutions like Lala's (page 18) and Mean-Eyed Cat (page
179), converted this former hair salon into a bar in 2014.

The black facade of the building is painted with white
bike wheels, and the walls of the tiny 800-square foot
interior are completely filled with black framed vintage
bicycle photos. Newsprint wallpaper, coppery ceiling
tiles, and Edison bulbs also harken back to a simpler
time. Overlapping bike wheels are suspended above
dark wooden picnic tables on the dog-friendly patio,
and a bike is suspended above a fountain made of beer
taps along the back wall.

Partner Max Moreland says the patio was originally wired for TVs, but they decided against adding them for fear that the screens would dominate the intimate space. And that decision has surely helped solidify them as the great community bar they are where, on any given day, the tables are filled with groups of friends, neighbors and co-workers immersed in conversation. While the bar is far too tiny for a kitchen, you can order tortas, tacos, bowls, and nachos from the neighbors at Austin Daily Press, then enjoy them here.

The bar first launched with a short list of well-made cocktails, named after all the partners' daughters, and Moreland says they intended to change the menu quarterly. But since the drinks were so well-received, and seemed to hit all the marks for the flavor profiles guests were seeking, they decided to keep these core creations and just add onto them with monthly specials. The most popular order is the Madison, a cozy variation on an Old Fashioned, made with rye whiskey, vanilla bean syrup, orange bitters, and clove. There's always 8 rotating beers on tap and The Wheel takes pride in sourcing some of the best from breweries both near and far, like AleSmith Brewing, Pinthouse Brewing, Firestone Walker Brewing Company, Prairie Artisan Ales, Champion Brewing Company, and Founders Brewing Co.

Though The Wheel is named after a Grateful Dead song, the music selection is quite diverse. The record player lives on a shelf behind the bar, with a "now playing" record display, and they host regular Bring Your Own Vinyl nights. On Monday nights, the bar lends out classic board games like Scattergories, Clue, Cranium, Monopoly, and Trivial Pursuit. The Wheel is proof that a great bar can rally the community together, no matter how small it may be. Of course, their reasonable prices don't hurt either. During the weekday happy hour, wells are just $3, tallboys are $3.50, and select signature cocktails drop to $8. Those who ride their bike can enjoy these prices well beyond the 4-7pm happy hour window. And there's always a $5 whiskey of the day, which can be used in any classic cocktail for a $3 upcharge.

"I think it's the perfect neighborhood bar," says Moreland. "It offers everything you could ever want in a tiny little space."

SAZERAC

Beyond the menu of signature creations, any bartender at The Wheel will be able to whip up a well-made classic cocktail for you. And with over 84 whiskies behind the bar to choose from, the brown classics tend to be the most popular. The New Orleans-born Sazerac, created by Creole apothecarist Antoine Peychaud in 1838, is thought to be the oldest known American cocktail. It was originally made with French cognac and a dash of absinthe, which evolved into rye and an absinthe rinse. But when absinthe was banned in 1912 for its hallucinogenic properties, Peychaud's Bitters were used in its place.

1 sugar cube or 1 tsp. sugar

3-4 dashes Peychaud's Bitters

2 oz. rye

¼ oz. absinthe

Lemon twist, to garnish

1. Muddle the sugar and the bitters in a mixing glass.

2. Add a few ice cubes to the glass and use a bar spoon to stir in the rye until chilled.

3. Pour the absinthe into an Old Fashioned glass, rotate the glass until coated, and discard any excess.

4. Strain the drink into the glass, express the lemon oils over it, and garnish with the twist.

TECHO MEZCALERIA

2201 Manor Road
Austin, TX 78722

Aurelio and Rosa Torres opened Mi Madre's, Manor Road's iconic Tex-Mex restaurant, in 1990 with five tables and a to-go counter for breakfast and lunch, expanding the space and menu as demand grew. Their son, Edgar Torres, met his wife Christina at the Culinary Institute of America and, after a stint living in San Diego, they decided to return to Austin to help with the family business. When they realized the neighborhood really needed a pub with great food, they opened School House Pub in front of Mi Madre's in 2013.

Two years after that, they decided to utilize another spot on the property. The space nestled above Mi Madre's—and accessible through a staircase in School House Pub's yard—used to be an efficiency Edgar's brother lived in before it became an office for the business. But they knew the space had more potential.

"Edgar brought me up there and said, 'What do you think about a rooftop mezcal bar?'" remembers Christina. "I agreed, but only if we could do cocktails. I was still warming up to mezcal during that time, and cocktails make mezcal more approachable until you dive in and fall in love like we have. Edgar was born in Mexico and the first alcohol he ever tasted was mezcal!"

They named the space Techo, which means "rooftop" in Spanish, and relished in taking their time to design the space, sourcing much of the decor in Mexico. They had a beautiful, rounded hand-carved wooden door custom-installed and laid blue and white talavera tiles on the ceiling, which really opens up the intimate space. A romantic mood is set with flickering veladoras and vintage light fixtures hanging from the ceiling. The brick side of the bar features a little candlelit alcove with Virgin of Guadalupe tile and a table for two. The wood side features vintage Mexican-made artwork, like a print declaring "El mezcal no te emborracha te pone mágico" ("Mezcal doesn't make you drunk, it makes you magical"). But the centerpiece is a stained glass depicting a mezcalero harvesting agave that Edgar commissioned an artist in his hometown of Saltillo to create.

An outdoor patio features black wrought iron tables and chairs, the perfect setting for enjoying their mezcal frozen guava margaritas, which drop to just $7 during happy hour (Tuesday though Friday 5-7pm and all day Sunday). Or choose from one of their signature cocktails, which rotate seasonally. I love the Otoño, made with sotol, serrano chile, lime, maguey sap, and a housemade spiced black cherry syrup. The bar features over 70 different types of agave spirits, leaning heavy

on mezcal, with a curation of tequila and lesser known spirits like sotol and raicilla and bacanora— plus Uruapan charanda (rum) and Abasolo whisky made from ancestral corn.

"We hand pick everything that goes on our back shelves," says Christina. "We try and showcase the love and hard work put into the bottles."

EL TAMAL

This winter, the team created a cocktail with the essence of a tamal, which they accomplished by incorporating Mi Madre's carnitas. After braising the seasoned pork for hours, they use the fat to fat-wash the Illegal mezcal overnight, which gives it a complex flavor and smooth mouthfeel. Nixta, a gently sweet Mexican liqueur made from ancestral corn, rounds out the cocktail with that distinct flavor of nixtamal, and Ancho Reyes provides just the right amount of spice and smoke.

2 oz. Fat-washed Ilegal Reposado

½ oz. Nixta liquor

½ oz. Ancho Reyes

Chile de árbol, to garnish

Corn husk, to garnish

1. Stir all three ingredients with ice in a cocktail shaker with a bar spoon.
2. Strain over one big ice cube in a rocks glass.
3. Garnish with a corn husk and chile de árbol.

Fat-Washed Illegal Reposado: Mi Madre's makes 20-pound batches of carnitas at a time. Season and prepare the pork according to your preference and then refrigerate, letting the fat separate. Remove the fat and heat it on a stovetop until just melted. Add 24 ounces of mezcal to 12 ounces of carnitas fat. Refrigerate overnight and then quickly fine-strain to remove fat.

THE SKYLARK LOUNGE

2039 Airport Boulevard
Austin, TX 78722

If you didn't know any better, you'd walk into Skylark Lounge and assume it had been there for decades. And that's exactly what owner Johnny LaTouf hopes you'd think.

"For about 30 years, it was the Airport Bar & Grill, a storied bar and grill for the movers and shakers of Austin's Black community," explains LaTouf. The native Austinite understands the importance of preserving pieces of the city's cultural history— particularly in East Austin, where he spent most of his time growing up and owned several businesses through the years before getting into commercial real estate.

When he contacted the owner of the 1960s lumber yard about purchasing the building, it was operating as a divey gay bar called Bernadette's. Though the property wasn't for sale, he did end up investing in the business and, when the manager decided to turn to other projects, he was given the opportunity to run operations. Having no experience in hospitality, he was hesitant, but he agreed and saw potential to revive a cornerstone of the East Austin creative community. He had also collected the advice of a few mentors through the years— namely the owners of the White Swan and the Victory

Grill, two historic East Austin bars, who had taken him under their wings.

"L.D. Davis of the White Swan told me, 'Johnny, a bar on the eastside is like an AM station; you've got to tune it in just right. One way or another and you're going to get too much static, so you've got to make those turns really easy to get the right sound'." he recalls. "I always remembered that, so I knew I didn't want to come in like other bar owners and do a big renovation."

Instead, he used all the original furniture, including handmade bar stools, and pulled some decor out of storage boxes in the back, before launching Skylark Lounge in 2013. The bar's dark ceiling, walls, and floor are lit by blue lights along the bar side, and red candles and lamps create a contrasting glow along the booth side. He also expanded the smoker-friendly backyard with mismatched vintage patio furniture, fans, and a fire pit. The bar is not only a nod to juke joints of the past, but a love letter to Austin too. The blinking Airport Boulevard-facing board announcing each night's headliners came from the now-shuttered campus-area I Luv Video, and signs from other old Austin businesses can be found throughout the space, alongside old show flyers and retro posters Skylark designs for performing musicians who play on their back corner stage.

"Since it had only been two things in the last 30 years—a gay bar and a bar that catered to the East Side African American community—I decided to try to bring both back since they'd both been there," he says. He sought out Miss Margaret Wright, a respected Black singer and pianist who had played all over town in her long career, from the Driskill Hotel to the Paramount Theater to gay bars. She went on to continue performing there weekly until she passed away right at the start of the pandemic. LaTouf largely attributes the crowd Skylark attracted to Wright's wide reach. "What we became known for, besides our music, was the diversity of who we were and how everyone got along," he says. "We had rich people, poor people, Black people, white people, gay people, straight people."

Since opening, Skylark Lounge has gone on to feature mainly blues, soul, R&B, and jazz musicians like Soul Man Sam, Birdlegg, and Miss Lavelle White, plus up-and-comers like Brian Scartocci, Goldie Pipes, and Billie

Bravo. The Soul Supporters started off playing here before they became the Black Pumas' rhythm section, and Charley Crockett used to also grace this stage — and LaTouf says he'll still stop by to play a surprise late night show every now and then.

Skylark closed for two years during the height of the pandemic, and was one of the last bars to reopen in November 2022, introducing a new cocktail program of classics and signature creations like the Skylark 77, a spin on a French 77, made with lime juice instead of lemon, and Blues on the Green, Malibu Rum, pineapple, and lime layered over blue curaçao. LaTouf remains close with his now-ex wife Mary Ellen, who books musicians and assists with management. All three of their kids have worked behind the bar—Christian and Brooklyn still do— as well as LaTouf's brother Terry. And he is proud to note that they welcome community birthday parties and celebrations but have turned down every buyout offer because he'd never want to turn away his regulars.

"This is really not about money," he says. "It's about curating a space that's going to stand for the neighborhood, building up relationships with everyone, and providing a stage presence for Black musicians."

More Locally Loved MLK and Manor Road Bars and Breweries:

SOUR DUCK MARKET
1814 E Martin Luther King Jr Boulevard, Austin, TX 78702

BAR TOTI
2113 Manor Road, Austin, TX 78722

SCHOOL HOUSE PUB
2207 Manor Road, Austin, TX 78722

THE BUTTERFLY BAR
2307 Manor Road, Austin, TX 78722

HAYMAKER
2310 Manor Road, Austin, TX 78722

BOBO'S SNACK BAR
3850 Airport Boulevard, Austin, TX 78722

ODDWOOD BREWING
3108 Manor Road, Austin, TX 78723

BATCH CRAFT BEER & KOLACHES
3220 Manor Road, Austin, TX 78723

MOONTOWER CIDER COMPANY
1916 Tillery Street, Austin, TX 78723

ROSEWOOD AND WEBBERVILLE

It's easy to talk about all the fun restaurants and bars that have opened as Austin rapidly expands. But it would be a disservice to ignore the elephant in the room—gentrification—and how it is connected to the city's growth. In 1928, Austin laid out a city planning initiative that sought to segregate the city through redlining, the federally sanctioned denial of services to residents in primarily non-white neighborhoods. Since the city couldn't directly force Austin's Black residents to move, they instead left them with no choice by removing essential resources. They closed down schools, parks, and hospitals in Wheatsville and Clarksville—then predominantly Black neighborhoods—and relocated them east of downtown. Expelled from the mainstream economic, social, and political discourse of Austin, the residents of the Eastside created their own microcosm. Black-owned businesses opened despite the many challenges that came with segregation, like zero access to bank loans or credit and extreme neighborhood zoning restrictions. Both 11th and 12th Streets were particularly important to the community, not only because of the churches, retail shops, convenience stores, barber shops, and restaurants located along those roads, but for the juke joints where local and touring blues and jazz acts played. These bars were part of a larger network of music venues known as the Chitlin' Circuit, created so that Black musicians could safely travel and play music during segregation. One instrumental venue, The Victory Grill, still stands on East 11th Street, painted with a mural of its founder Johnny Holmes alongside pianist Roosevelt "Grey Ghost" Williams, the first musician to play there.

As East Austin gains popularity, that growth is fueled primarily by white residents, and minorities continue to be displaced due to sky-rocketing property taxes and a severe lack of affordable housing. Though the neighborhood has already changed drastically, some remnants of the past remain. The neighborhood is home to Huston-Tillotson University, the city's historically Black private university. Sam's BBQ, open since 1956, is still serving brisket and, just down the street, Ideal Barber Shop has been keeping the community trimmed since 1947. Kenny Dorham's Backyard is an outdoor music venue located right near the legendary jazz trumpeter and composer's last home in Austin. The George Washington Carver Museum honors the history and contribution of Black Austinites and the Texas Music Museum captures the legacies of the blues and jazz musicians who helped to establish Austin as the "Live Music Capital." Change may be inevitable, but it's essential that neighborhood revitalization comes with cultural preservation and an inclusion of the people who made this city what it is.

SAHARA LOUNGE

1413 Webberville Road
Austin, TX 78721

I've been frequenting Sahara Lounge since it was TC's Lounge, a little shanty that would pack to capacity for the Little Elmore Reed Blues Band's insanely popular Monday night residency. TC's was a Bring Your Own Liquor establishment, and the bar sold set-ups of mixers and ice, which melted almost immediately on the steamy dancefloor. There was always a crockpot of chicken and dumplings—or a similar comfort food—on the bar and focused games of pool happening no matter how loud or crowded of a night it was.

When the space changed hands in 2011, just as Austin was going through a lot of drastic development, I, like many others, started to mourn the loss of an institutional dive bar. But TC (Thomas Perkins) was excited to move on after 33 years in the business, and musician Eileen Bristol, her son Topaz McGarrigle, of Austin's popular psychedelic band Golden Dawn Arkestra, and her bandmate, multi-instrumentalist Ibrahim Aminou of Afrobeat band Zoumountchi were committed to preserving this eastside gem. Beyond adding a liquor license, making some much-needed improvements to the bathroom, and decorating with relics brought back from Eileen and Ibrahim's visits throughout Africa, not much has changed.

When you first enter the structure, originally built in 1962, you'll be met with a melange of lamps, tapestries, tribal sculptures and instruments. Prayer flags are strung above the bar, and several large jars of infusions sit on a nearby shelf. A bookshelf presents a collection of well-loved books for the borrowing plus tarot cards and a backgammon board. The bar's low ceilings are painted the same maroon color as the walls, and the glow of twinkling string lights and billiard lamps light the windowless space, giving it a basement rec room feel.

"People feel at home in here, whether they're from Brazil or Japan," says Bristol. "If you imagine everything we do in a sterile building, it just wouldn't be the same. This building has really got a lot of magic to it, a lot of music in the walls."

The stage features music most nights of the week, including a weekly Africa Nightwith house band Zoumountchi and vibrant dance floor community, plus popular Latin nights and disco, funk, and soul-driven Ladies Nights on the third Friday of each month. The expanded back patio, now with a fire pit and long communal tables, means more space for socializing with the kind and interesting people I always seem to meet out there.

KING BEE

1906 E 12th Street
Austin, TX 78702

In a city of perpetual change, it's refreshing when growth comes with respect for those who paved the way. The Legendary White Swan was a historic East Austin club that opened on East 12th Street in the 1960s, featuring mainly blues, soul, jazz, and R&B. It was also one of Austin's Green Book properties that provided a safe space for Black musicians during an era of segregation.

When the Swan closed in 2014, hospitality vets Billy and Colette Hankey took over operations that same year, keeping the bar as close to the original as possible and naming it after a Slim Harpo song, "I'm a King Bee." They ran the bar for six years, becoming known as a divey cocktail destination with an impressive mezcal collection and one of the best kept pizza secrets in town. But when the duo decided to shutter and move on to other pursuits early during the pandemic, Pouring with Heart —a hospitality group that runs award-winning bars in California, Colorado, and Texas, including Half Step (page 238)—took over.

"King Bee exemplifies what we are all about: a neighborhood bar for everyone," says director of operations Steven Robbins. "We were so privileged to be considered for the honor of carrying the torch. I myself, like many of us, was a regular since day one. I even worked bar shifts at King Bee during the early days and have always been in love with the bar and what it represents."

The bar still features well-made cocktails, which rotate whenever the bartenders feel inspired to mix it up, leaning toward classics and riffs on classics. A board lists specials which range from silly shots to seasonal bangers plus two draft cocktails and a frozen drink, which may very well be the frozen Bees Knees Billy Hankey became known for when he first launched King Bee. Beer ranges from local and craft to cheap and cold, and that's the kind of high-low approach Pouring with Heart uses to keep things accessible for everyone.

"We certainly try to make a good drink but don't identify as a cocktail bar," says Robbins. "We consider ourselves 'cocktail adjacent,' as we serve a shot of Mellow Corn and a Lone Star with the same pride as a damn good Old Fashioned or Negroni variation."

The hospitality group renovated the bathrooms and made some very minor cosmetic and mechanical repairs, but otherwise continued to honor the historic site by making as few changes as possible. The dog-friendly patio remains no-frills but has been updated with some planters and umbrellas. They added a pool table back to the spacious interior, and painted an eight ball on the building's glossy black facade much like the one on the Swan's original sign. They gave the place a fresh coat of black paint to maintain its signature interior vibe, which Robbins describes as "dark and moody with an inherent warmth that only comes from decades of laughter and tears."

The back wall of the stage still boasts the Louis Armstrong mural created by renowned local muralist Federico Archuleta. And while music has always remained an important part of King Bee, they now host live shows nightly, from blues and jazz to indie and metal. Resident musician—and "unofficial mascot and king of the bar," according to Robbins—Mac Mcintosh grew up in the neighborhood and used to dream of playing on the stage. Now he and the Michael Hale Trio light the stage up every Sunday for King Bee's weekly "Date Night."

"The Legendary White Swan hosted countless musicians over the years from James Brown and Nancy Wilson to Etta James and so many others," says Robbins. "The space holds a particular magic in the walls that you can feel when watching a show, which makes it so special and absolutely irreplaceable."

ADELITA

Steven Robbins created this cocktail at Half Step in 2016, but now serves it at King Bee. He was playing around with a gin cocktail called the Old Maid, which is essentially an Eastside cocktail on the rocks, and tried adding in Aperol. One night, he created a drink for a margarita-loving regular by swapping gin for tequila. "I started calling it an Abuelita in regard to the Old Maid reference but a friend said, 'No way, that damn thing's got way too much kick for that name,'" so I changed it to the Adelita. After that it became a very popular back pocket cocktail."

Mint

½ oz. simple syrup

1 oz. fresh lime juice

1½ oz. still strength tequila (King Bee uses Tapatio 110)

½ oz. Aperol

Pinch of mint, to garnish

Three cucumber wheels, to garnish

1. Muddle the mint, simple syrup and lime in a cocktail shaker before adding the tequila and Aperol.

2. Shake and strain over ice in a rocks glass.

3. Garnish with cucumber wheels and a small bouquet of mint.

NICKEL CITY

1133 E 11th Street
Austin, TX 78702

Step inside Nickel City and you'll get the feeling you're in a bar that's been there for a very long time. And technically speaking, you are—in fact, the space houses the longest continuously run bar in the whole city. Long before Nickel City opened in 2017, Pike's Place opened just a few days after Prohibition was repealed—but it is thought to have been a speakeasy long before that. Through the years, it took on different names and owners. During the 1940s and 1950s, it was part of the Chitlin' Circuit, and in 1965, it became the Longbranch Inn and ran continuously as such until 2016. My first memories of the bar were playing pool at its one dimly lit table and cramming in with what must've been an illegal number of people to see some very cozy, rowdy shows during South by Southwest.

Bar veteran Travis Tober, who now has 25 years of service industry experience under his belt, worked in New York, West Palm Beach, and Las Vegas before moving to Austin in 2011, intent on opening his own bar. When he heard about the available historic space on East 11th, he jumped on the opportunity, making some interior choices to brighten up the space while maintaining its blue-collar approachability.

"I always call this my grandpa's bar," says Tober. "When my friends come down here, they're like, 'This is like every dump we ever hung out at!' We call it 'rust belt chic' here."

His inspiration for Nickel City came from his hometown Buffalo's boilermaker bars, which notoriously open up at 8 a.m. for the third shift workers who install and maintain boilers overnight. Two long window panes at the front let in enough daytime light to illuminate the red walls, red and green checkerboard floors, and yellow vinyl booths. The 24-foot vintage oak back bar, which came from the lobby bar of the Driskill before it was brought over to the Longbranch, lives on at Nickel City. A marquee, glowing above a cigarette vending machine and a Simpsons pinball machine, counts the ounces of Coors they've sold since opening.

And while, yes, you can get a Miller High Life pony bottle for $2, you'd be remiss not to work your way through the always-changing cocktail menu, which is split into: Well-Known (classics), Lesser-Known (inventions made by industry friends at bars around the world), Unknown (creations of their own), and Tiki selections. Nickel City also boasts over 300 whiskey labels, including the largest collection of single barrel whiskey in the state, carrying anywhere from 4-12 on any given day. They've developed a cult following for their rich and creamy frozen Irish coffee, which was inspired by the versions found at the Erin Rose and Molly's in New Orleans.

"We're a place where a line cook sits next to a stock broker," says Tober. "You can come in here and have a beer and a shot—or a couple of them—without breaking the bank, but you can also spend $600 on 4 ounces of whiskey if you want. So it's an even playing field. We have a little bit for everybody by design, to make it an interesting place to hang out."

A window labeled "Cash Only" in the back of the bar serves as a (cash-only, naturally) site for bar pop-ups, with money going to different organizations each time. As a continued homage to the rust belt, Travis partnered with the Hunt brothers, who own VIA 313, a local chain of Detroit-style pizza, to open Delray Cafe, a trailer serving Detroit-style sliders and coneys in Nickel City's side yard. They're also one of the only places in town who do Buffalo wings the right way—weighed by the pound, brined for 24 hours and fried to a perfect crisp.

As if all that isn't enough, the bar dresses up as Moe's Tavern from The Simpsons for Halloween each year, and decks the halls in tiki for Christmastime. And if you happen to visit during a Buffalo Bills game? I'm not sure how I could possibly prepare you for that...

TEMPORARY FRIENDS

This is one of Travis Tober's favorite creations from the Unknown cocktails Nickel City makes in-house. He created this one in honor of their Irish whiskey rep, a "temporary friend" who was only planning to stay in town for 18 months before moving onto the next destination. Chamomile tea, elderflower liqueur, and Bittercube's Bolivar Bitters give this drink a gently floral, aromatic profile not commonly found in whiskey drinks.

1¾ oz. Lost Irish Whiskey

¾ oz. fresh lemon juice

½ oz. chamomile tea-infused honey (2 parts honey to 1 part chamomile tea)

¼ oz. elderflower liqueur

3 dashes Bittercube Bolivar Bitters

Absinthe, for rinsing

Mint, to garnish

1. Combine all of the ingredients in a shaker tin and add ice.
2. Shake vigorously for 10 seconds.
3. Double-strain cocktail over fresh cubed ice into an absinthe-rinsed rocks glass.
4. Garnish with mint and serve.

KITTY COHEN'S

2211 Webberville Road, #3548
Austin, TX 78702

I don't care who you are or how long you've lived in Austin: there comes a point in the summer where you become simply incapacitated by the heat. Enter Kitty Cohen's, the only place on the east side where you can sip frozen drinks while submerged in water—unless, you know, you own a pool... in which case, I salute you.

I used to live just a couple blocks from the little shanty of a structure called H&H Tavern, which had been in operation for around 30 years. When the owners decided to sell, Jeremy Murray and his partners, who'd owned the now-shuttered Blackheart on Rainey Street, as well as the nearby High Noon and Proof and Cooper in Dripping Springs, took over the lease in 2015.

At first, they turned it into a little neighborhood bar called 2211, named after the street address on Webberville Road, not making too many changes to the longtime local dive. But the bar entrepreneurs saw more potential in the property—and particularly its spacious backyard. After a year, they rebranded and launched as Kitty Cohen's, a kitschy cocktail lounge with a tropical oasis in the backyard.

"They all have really free-spirited, independent matriarchal women in their lives," explains Jessica Tantillo Murray, Jeremy's wife. "For some it was their mothers, and others it was their aunts or grandmothers, so they wanted to memorialize those women with a bar.... one

with a really beautiful patio with a kind of tacky, fun interior."

But Kitty Cohen's is best known for the long, two-foot-deep pool on the patio, originally intended for foot soaking, though Jessica says they've seen it all, from people skinny dipping to folks showing up with beach bags and pool accessories for the day. Frosé is the summer drink of choice, though there are always two frozen options spinning all year long, which is great for those 80 degree December days. In lieu of a food truck, they use their outside bar to host chef pop-ups, and it has served as an incubator for new concepts, from Mama Kong's Cambodian food to Che Cazzo's inventive Italian to Le Beef grass-fed burgers.

The cool blue interior exudes thrift-store chic, with highlights like wheelie casino chairs, a sparkly gold padded bar arm rest, and bathrooms decked out with flamingos and pin-up photos. Guests can choose from cheekily named cocktails, like Sex Panther, or opt for $2 Lone Star or throw down on a $40 shot of Pappy Van Winkle. And for the last four years, the bar has transformed into a Hanukkah pop-up for the month of December, with glittering blue decor and themed food and drink.

"From the second you walk through that gate, we want you to feel a bit of escapism," says Tantillo Murray. "It's that feeling you're in someone's home and everyone is welcome and comfortable. Most of all, we want it to be really fun."

SEX PANTHER

The Sex Panther, now one of the longest running drinks on their menu, was created by previous Kitty Cohen's bar manager Rachel Dancer. "We are always inspired by the feminine energy of the bar and sexy names lend themselves to our drinks," says Jessica Tantillo Murray. " I love the smile it brings to customers' faces when they order and say, 'I'll take a Sex Panther please.'"

1¾ oz. Mezcal Unión Joven

¾ oz. passion fruit syrup (Liber & Co's version will work great for this)

½ oz. lemon juice

2-3 dashes bitters

Mint, to garnish

Dried lemon wheel, to garnish

1. Build the cocktail in a shaker with ice.

2. Shake ingredients, then pour over ice into a rocks glass.

3. Garnish with a dried lemon wheel and mint.

More Locally Loved Rosewood and Webberville Bars:

CORK & SCREW
2907 E 12th Street, Austin, TX 78702

BIRDIE'S
2944 E 12th Street, Unit A, Austin, TX 78702

FULL CIRCLE BAR
1810 E 12th Street, Austin, TX 78702

SKINNY'S OFF TRACK BAR
1806 E 12th Street, Austin, TX 78702

OUTER HEAVEN DISCO CLUB
1808 E 12th Street, Austin, TX 78702

SADDLE UP
1309 Rosewood Avenue, Austin, TX 78702

MURRAY'S TAVERN
2316 Webberville Road, Austin, TX 78702

THE LOST WELL
2421 Webberville Road, Austin, TX 78702

THE CAVALIER
2400 Webberville Road, Suite A, Austin, TX 78702

EAST 7TH STREET AND GOVALLE

Although East Austin has been shifting into its current state since the early aughts, the main thoroughfare of East 7th Street hasn't seen too much development until more recently. Finished in 2016, The 7East building, home to APT 115 (page 106), was one of the earlier eastside buildings to bill itself as "luxury living," while surrounded by a hodgepodge of check-cashing establishments, pawn shops, and gas stations. Perhaps because it hasn't been completely over-run by developers, the street also boasts some long-standing family-owned businesses, such as Casa Colombia, Los Comales, a botánica called Green & White Grocery, and Joe's Bakery, a Tex-Mex diner and panadería that was named an America's Classic Restaurant by the James Beard Foundation in 2023. More businesses started to open on the street in the last decade, like Salt & Time Butcher Shop and its adjacent wine shop, the inclusive Cute Nail Studio, and Gabrielas Downtown, who acquired neighboring Revival

Driftwood

Hays

Coffee to save it during the pandemic. Even more recently, the eastern-most stretch of the street, from Pleasant Valley to 183, has developed into a little pocket of bars, from laidback watering holes like Kinda Tropical and Sunny's Backyard to more upscale cocktail concepts like Holiday (page 113) and Bosses Office (page 109).

Several blocks north of 7th Street, the mainly residential Govalle neighborhood has bloomed with some great community spaces like Canopy Austin, an art studio center that often opens its doors to the public, and the popular climbing center East Austin Bouldering Project as well as the viral kawaii dessert shop OMG Squee and Springdale General, a mixed-use complex where you can find hand rolls, French pastries, stationary, or pilates. Head a few blocks further south on Springdale, and you will encounter another little pocket. When Justine's Brassiere (page 118) opened here in 2009, the surrounding area was completely industrial, and remained that way for years. Now, Koko's Bavarian, De Nada Cantina, and Central Machine Works have become neighbors, and an influx of art studios are sprinkled throughout too.

APT 115

2025 E 7th Street
Austin, TX 78702

Plenty of bars have been called homey, but that descriptor is more fitting for APT 115 than most. That's because the intimate wine bar and restaurant is set in an actual ground-level apartment unit in the 7East building on East 7th Street. Originally built as a live-work space, Joe Pannenbacker took over the lease and opened as a wine bar in March 2018.

Pannenbacker first got into wine in his early twenties while working as a server in high-end restaurants to supplement his income as a bassist in bands like Semihelix and Think No Think. He was also bit by the travel bug along the way and has collected much of his food and beverage knowledge from eating and drinking around the world. Operation Dagger, a Singapore speakeasy that shuttered during the pandemic, is one of his many global inspirations.

"You walked to this back door that was marked with, like, hobo permanent marker and you then open it and you're like, 'Am I supposed to be in here?'" Pannenbacker remembers. "But then the cocktails were really cool and there's no labels on any of the bottles because they make their own spirits. I guess I was inspired by the unexpectedness of it, and that element lends itself to APT 115's quirkiness."

While APT 115 isn't by any means a speakeasy, it has somehow earned a reputation as one because of its unexpected location. Guests often refer to it as the "secret wine bar," which always gives Pannenbacker a chuckle. "We've got to be the only 'speakeasy' with a neon sign out front," he says. The 737 square foot space is home to over 400 different labels of small-production wine made with minimal winemaker intervention, but don't expect to see the same trendy, natty labels you'll find everywhere else.

"When I first opened, I kind of went heavy France and California, just because I felt that those were places that were pushing the envelope but still making high quality wine that were classic of the region," says Pannenbacker, who has expanded the current wine list to 48 pages, spanning all six continents that produce wine, with a focus on lesser-known regions and grapes.

He first opened with a selection of cheese and charcuterie, cut-to-order on a vintage meat slicer, but mid-pandemic he started to develop the menu to stay open as a restaurant. With a growing interest in a food program, he decided to up the ante by granting a well-established chef creative license to develop the menu. In 2021, he brought on Charles Zhuo, whose resume includes Barley Swine in Austin and Minibar in

DC, and he created a 10-course tasting menu, using products sourced from local farms and ranches. Guests can opt to add a wine pairing, which always comes with sparkling, white, rose, orange, red, and sweet wine selections. But unlike most restaurants with tasting menus, you can also opt to just enjoy bar snacks, like root vegetable tots with cilantro ranch— and they'll open just about any bottle in the house for you to enjoy by the glass.

"We're not really exactly like anything else—we're our own thing," says Pannenbacker, easily spotted with his wild curly hair and a vivid printed button-down, while making rounds to excitedly talk with each table about his latest favorite bottles or flip the record on the turntable. The APT 115 plays nothing but vinyl—no DJs, no requests, just full albums all the way through—and the collection ranges from Supertramp to Slayer, David Bowie to Tammy Wynette, Cocteau Twins to Run The Jewels.

While Pannenbacker might not appear to be your average sommelier, APT 115 isn't your typical wine bar either. The tiny 22-seat space features robin's egg blue walls and another accented by patterned wallpaper designed by Brian Eno. Green 1970s-era Herman Miller bucket seats mix with pink scratched-up vintage metal lawn chairs and heavy navy classroom chairs tagged as "property of Texas School for the Deaf." The space is illuminated by custom rope lighting designed by Luke Lamp Co., and shelves built against floor-to-ceiling windows display plants, well-worn books and estate sale tchotchkes, ranging from teapots to ashtrays and clocks to candleholders. A vintage globe stands as a reminder of Pannenbacker's travels, both past and future.

"But you don't need to travel halfway around the world to have a life-changing experience," he says. "Sometimes things in your own backyard can be the most memorable."

BOSSES OFFICE

3223 E 7th Street
Austin, TX 78702

After having their restaurant broken into four times in two weeks, Adam Jacoby and Kris Swift were faced with a decision to either call it quits or creatively problem-solve the challenges being thrown their way.

As restaurateurs who'd already successfully run two restaurants, Jacoby's Restaurant & Mercantile and Grizzelda's, through a pandemic, these life- and business-partners are no strangers to challenges. In April 2021, they expanded their JRG Hospitality empire with a new concept, Swift Pizza Co., just a half mile north of their other two on East 7th Street. The structure had been built in 1975 by Paul and Teresa Saldaña to house The Texas Café, and then Michael and Margarita Raupe opened a burger joint called Chumikal's in the space in 1989, closing it to retire at the end of 2018.

Swift Pizza Co. had brought some much-needed pizza to the Govalle neighborhood and business was ramping up, but after their fourth break-in in October, during which their point-of-sale system was destroyed and an aquarium smashed, they felt broken, both physically and emotionally. They decided to shutter Swifty's, use the kitchen to prep for their other restaurants so there was almost always someone on-site, and open a cocktail bar in the space instead.

"In order to be a real boss in life, whether it's to yourself or the other people that surround you, you need to be

able to take some of the most challenging and darkest moments and be able to see the opportunity in them to change and evolve," says Swift. "In this case, we started talking about people who motivated and inspired us, people we really looked up to and what they stood for, and how they acted—and this is what inspired Bosses Office."

Creative director and co-owner Kris Swift, a veteran of HGTV *Design Star*'s seventh season, set to work transforming the space with his keen eye for design. A coat of black paint on the brick exterior, and a neon sign above the door, makes for a mysterious entrance to an instantly chic, soothingly dark space.

"When you enter our doors I want the rest of the world to melt away into the background," says Swift. "We strive to create an environment that allows you to connect with new and old friends with zero stress."

Mid-century modern furniture, vintage desk lamps, and hanging ferns give the bar an executive feel, softened with shimmery pillows and flickering candlelight, plus playful touches like a bookshelf-printed accent wall, a vintage disco ball from Berlin, and framed vintage car ads against a leaf-printed wall. The attention to detail in lighting fixtures, particularly the dreamy vintage chandelier at the entrance, matches the attention to detail in glassware, from the Depression glass tumblers to the flat-rimmed ribbed coupes.

Since the bar is a celebration of bosses, from all walks of life, who have inspired all the team members, each drink on the menu honors a different one. There's the Anthony Bourdain, a complex and brooding riff on a Manhattan, which comes wafted in smoke made from a proprietary blend of cherrywood and coffee. Or the Willie Nelson, a tiki drink made smokey with mezcal and served in a bong-shaped glass with a flaming lime. And perhaps most unexpected is the Janis Joplin, a uniquely sweet and savory concoction made from mushroom and thyme-infused cognac and lavender-infused honey stirred with black walnut bitters and served neat, garnished with the cross section of a mushroom.

A menu of snacks and small plates features decadent offerings like beer-cheese stuffed pretzels, Parmesan truffle fries, and caviar served with crème fraîche and kettle chips. And the perfectly sweet-salty-umami truffled Chex mix gifted to each table is so positively addictive, I'm certain it's created many a regular guest already. Looks like it's going to be another late night at the Office.

CHARLES DARWIN

"This cocktail is actually inspired by Jacoby's, our ranch-to-table concept," says Beverage Director Taryn Epperson of this herbal, savory Gimlet variation. "As a bartender there, I worked closely with our chef and learned a great deal and was inspired to take a more culinary approach to building cocktails. Once the drink took shape, it was a no-brainer to use the natural, earthy elements of this cocktail to honor one of the greatest contributors—bosses, if you will—to biology."

2 oz. chopped fennel bulb

2 oz. arugula

2 oz. Aviation gin

¾ oz. fresh lime

½ oz. simple syrup

Fennel frond, to garnish

Lemon wedge, to garnish

1. Muddle the fennel and arugula in the cocktail shaker to release the oils in both.

2. Combine all of the ingredients in the cocktail tin, add ice and shake vigorously.

3. Strain into a glass over ice.

4. Garnish with a vibrant fennel frond and lemon for a pop of color.

HOLIDAY

5020 E 7th Street
Austin, TX 78702

Sure, long vacations are great. But sometimes a brief respite from everyday life can be just as replenishing. Madonna knows it, and so does cocktail savant Erin Ashford.

"A bar should be transportive," says Ashord. "A place where you can slow down and enjoy the company you are with, as well as a chance to imbibe and indulge a little more into drinks and food than you might at home during a busy work week."

After moving to Austin from Florida when she was 21, Ashford worked at some of the best bars in town before joining the team at award-winning Olamaie, where she graduated from bar manager to beverage director. That's where she met John DiCicco and Peter Klein, and the three became fast friends. DiCicco and Klein were station partners on the hot line before they became roommates. Their epic dinner parties featured spreads of food and drink served family-style, meant for grazing and sipping by candlelight in the backyard. The three decided to collaborate on a concept and began to think about what they personally wanted from their ideal bar.

"We didn't feel like there was a bar in town doing what we are striving to do," says Ashford. "Where can you eat a chef-made meal with a proper martini after 10:30 pm? Where can you walk in without a reservation on a Friday night? What bar could you go to that felt elevated and fancy but also easy and carefree? It just doesn't really exist."

They set out to create a bar with the hospitality of a top-tier restaurant. Service would be attentive but un-obtrusive. Though the focus would be on expertly-made cocktails, the same attention to detail would be paid to the food, which would be easily shareable and reminiscent of a cocktail party spread. And while most cocktail bars in town have a more dark and masculine design, Ashford wanted to create a space with a more feminine aesthetic, beautiful ambiance and a vibey playlist.

DiCicco had gone on to become a partner at Kinda Tropical, a neighborhood bar just down the street. As the Govalle neighborhood quickly started to grow, he had his eye on a neighboring 1950s gas station-turned auto body shop-turned used car lot. When another business backed out, they were able to secure the lease with the help of a broker. When Holiday opened on East 7th Street in March 2023, they had a line curved around the block to get in.

I still haven't been to Holiday after dark, but I feel like the space is designed to be experienced during the day, when sunshine floods in through the wide, black-rimmed windows. The breezy, white-walled interior features a light grey marble bar and tabletops paired with elegant, Scandinavian-looking wooden bar stools and light wooden chairs sourced from a local library. Interior designer Candice Bertalan of Tropic of Capricorn hand-tiled the coffee tables and crafted the bar's white pendant lights. Pops of color come from big cacti in large black clay pots, as well as a large portrait of a "Woman on Holiday" painted by local artist Ryan Camarillo.

Vintage glassware sourced from local shops provide elegant vessels for Ashford's creations, including a frozen Mexican martini, which comes in a glass with a green cactus stem. The menu has a strong focus on agave, amari, and gin, but it also doesn't ignore vodka (an oft-ignored spirit). Kástra Elión, a Greek vodka distilled from olives, adds salinity and depth to their "87 Club" signature martini, balanced with citrus from Old Tom gin and sweetness from Martini & Rossi Ambrato vermouth. Ashford became known for her perfectly balanced punch at Olamaie, so there's fittingly a punch cup at Holiday that changes weekly. Some recent offerings included bourbon, Aperol, orange liqueur, and lime topped with sparkling rose, and mezcal, mango liqueur, lemon, and cardamom bitters topped with ginger beer. There's also a well-curated list of beer and wine, plus several spirit-free offerings.

Klein's menu features refined classics with his own creative twist. Baguette and house-cultured butter is served with white and brown Spanish anchovies and a bright preserved lemon salsa verde, the perfect pairing with a bracing dry martini. Chicken liver mousse is given a sweet punch with white port gelee and strawberry green garlic mostarda. Crunchy zucchini fritters are dolloped with Parmesan aioli and sprinkled with smoked trout roe for an umami burst with each bite. A black-and white-sesame crusted pork schnitzel served over creamy herbed gribiche with lemony frisée is a symphony of balanced textures and flavors.

Like most holidays, you're not going to want this one to end.

LYCHEE MARTINI

Ashford knew she wanted to feature an entire martini section on the Holiday menu, and felt like a lychee martini would be fitting for the current 1990s resurgence. "Helen (Lai) and I workshopped this together and really got a kick out of putting it on draft at Holiday to make it carbonated," she says. Soho lychee liqueur gives the cocktail a natural tropical flavor without being overly sweet, while honeysuckle vodka adds a white flowery perfume and blanc vermouth lends rich vanilla notes and gives the drink some backbone.

1½ oz. Cathead Honeysuckle vodka

½ oz. Dolin Blanc vermouth

½ oz. Soho Lychee liqueur

½ oz. fresh lemon juice

¼ oz. simple syrup (1:1)

3 drops Saline Solution

1 splash sparkling water or Champagne

Lychee, to garnish

Cherry, to garnish

1. Add all ingredients to your shaker tin.

2. Fill tin with cubed ice and shake 20 times.

3. Double strain, using a Hawthorne and fine mesh strainer, into a stemmed glass such as a vintage coupe.

4. Top with a splash of sparkling water of champagne.

5. Garnish with a lychee and a cherry on a metal cocktail pick.

Saline Solution: Using a tea kettle, boil 2 cups water. Pour into a lidded jar or vessel. Add 1 teaspoon of salt to the hot water. Stir until completely dissolved. Let cool before covering. Keep stored at room temperature.

JUSTINE'S BRASSERIE

4710 E 5th Street
Austin, TX 78702

Now, I know Gen Z slang can get overused, but I really mean it when I say that Justine's is a whole vibe.

Known for its notoriously sceney late-night dining, this eastside brasserie is set in a little house that was built in 1937 and had a reputation for being "a place of bad behavior," according to owner Justine Gilcrease. Gilcrease met her now-husband Pierre Pelegrin while on a road trip through Austin several decades ago. The two fell in love and moved to Paris before making their way back to Austin, where they decided to open a bohemian brasserie.

"We both loved the idea of creating what we originally thought would be like our living room: a place for friends and artists to gather," Gilcrease remembers.

Chef Justin Huffman beautifully executes Justine's classic dishes—like garlicky escargots à la bourguignonne, perfect steak frites, rich French onion soup, hearty cassoulet — as well as a rotating menu of seasonal specials. There is, of course, a menu of French wine offerings, and they always offer reasonably priced house wine by the glass and carafe. A chalkboard in the bar displays a list of house cocktails, including the signature L'Enfant Terrible, designed by Olivier, one of the original bartenders who emigrated from France with Pelegrin. The baby-pink martini, which is quite like a botanical Cosmo, is made from Ketel One Citroen vodka, St-Germain, cranberry juice, and lime.

When designing the space, Gilcrease and Pelegrin took inspiration from the brasseries and bistros they would frequent in Paris, from the flickering neon sign at the

entrance to the Thonet bar stools inside. They even acquired the original brass bistro tables from Bar Hemingway at the Ritz Paris. The sultry, red-walled dining room is packed with framed art, much of it collected on their annual trips back to France, from a piece by French painter Henri de Toulouse-Lautrec to photos taken by Diane Arbus, André Kertész, and Andy Warhol. They only play records here, so the bartenders double as DJs and the back bar is also a vinyl library. The soundtrack might start with Lightnin' Hopkins, the patron saint of Texas blues, before transitioning to the French classics of Charles Aznavour or the eclectic sounds of Afro-pop duo Amadou & Mariam.

"It's also got a little Texas roadhouse, dive bar vibe, being a joint where many musicians come after their shows and tons of locals hang out, music is all-important," says Gilcrease, who has hosted many shows on the property, too, from Syrian wedding singer Omar Souleyman to zydeco pioneer Classie Ballou.

In the crackling space between the needle dropping and the music playing, you can hear the bar abuzz with a frenetic type of energy. Outside, you'll encounter a more chill, romantic vibe, particularly during colder months, when the stone patio is covered with cascading blue and red velveteen fabric to create the Winter Tent. Chandeliers illuminate each sumptuous fold, and marble tables, woven French bistro chairs, and guinguette string lights transport you to a place that feels more like the 20th arrondissement than an industrial part of East Austin.

"While it's a beautiful space, elegant and creative and a tiny bit luxurious, it's not an elitist place," says Gilcrease. "Justine's, from the day it opened, has been about welcoming everyone, and celebrating a true community, not a VIP society. The restaurant has a sense of humor and mischief and doesn't take itself too seriously, and genuinely holds its arms open to all of Austin."

The Justine's staff truly welcomes any excuse to dress up, whether it's an Oscars party, Bastille Day, or a Marquis de Sade-themed dinner party. And their New Year's Eve bash is easily the most decadent and debauched event in town. In years past, they've transformed the yard for a very different type of soiree, from a postmodern dreamland with neon palm trees to a psychedelic circus with trapeze artists and a ferris wheel. One year they installed 200 pine trees and imported 20,000 pounds of fake snow to build a Black Forest. Another year they built a neon-trimmed pagoda for a Kubla Khan-themed New Year's with a Shanghai market; that pagoda has now become a mirror-lined lounge where guests sip on cocktails, often waiting for a table or for their tintype portrait to process. Photobooth trailer Lumiere Tintype has called Justine's home for the last decade, and its beautifully ghostly tintype art pieces are the perfect keepsake to cap off an undoubtedly special night.

More Locally Loved East 7th Street and Govalle Bars and Breweries:

EASY TIGER EAST
1501 E 7th Street, Austin, TX 78702

KINDA TROPICAL
3501 E 7th Street, Austin, TX 78702

SUNNY'S BACKYARD
3526 E 7th Street, Austin, TX 78702

FRIENDS AND ALLIES BREWING
979 Springdale #124 Road, Austin, TX 78702

HI SIGN BREWING
730 Shady Lane, Austin, TX 78702

KOKO'S BAVARIAN
4715 E 5th Street, Austin, TX 78702

CENTRAL MACHINE WORKS
4824 E César Chávez Street, Austin, TX 78702

DE NADA CANTINA
4715 E César Chávez Street, Austin, TX 78702

LUSTRE PEARL EAST
114 Linden Street, Austin, TX 78702

EAST 6TH STREET

If you're going by the map, West 6th Street technically becomes East 6th Street after crossing Congress Avenue, where the block numbering starts over. However, when someone refers to East 6th Street, they are undoubtedly talking about the section of the street east of I-35. When the highway was constructed in the 1960s, it served as a border between the downtown and East Austin, which already had its own bars, restaurants, and shops frequented by the Hispanic majority populating the neighborhood.

In 2007, Randall Stockton and his wife Donya, who owned the Red River venue Beerland at the time, took over ownership of a dive bar and taqueria named Rio Rita, turning it into a coffee shop with cocktails. During the 2008 recession, a lot of the local businesses took a nosedive. Many new bars started taking over the leases of the older Tejano bars, changing the fabric of the neighborhood. Nearby on East 4th Street, The Scoot Inn, which once had sawdust on the floor and a jukebox broadcasting mariachi and ranchera, became a live music venue. Whisler's (page 133) opened in the spot where Rabbit's Lounge, a

Driftwood

Hays

124

hub for Chicano politics, once stood. Family-owned Tex-Mex restaurants like Nuevo Leon's and Dario's shut down one by one. But Tamale House East, opened in 1958, is still owned by the Valera family and thriving. The iconic Cisco's Restaurant & Bakery, opened in 1950 by Rudy Cisneros, still stands on the corner of East 6th and Chicon, preserved by a group that includes Rudy's grandson Matt Cisneros and Will Bridges, the owner of Deep Eddy Cabaret (page 182). And right across the street from it, La Perla (page 147) is the last remaining Tejano dive bar on the entirety of East 6th Street and Johnnie's Antiques, still housed in its original 1918 building, opens each Wednesday for a few hours.

But beyond that, the street is virtually unrecognizable these days, flanked on each side by luxury lofts and hotels. While there are still some dives and food trucks along the strip, there are increasingly more cocktail bars and higher end restaurants like Suerte, Vixen's Wedding, and Canje. The "new wave" of Austin bars that opened in the mid-2000s, like Shangri-La, The Liberty, and Violet Crown Social Club, is now seeing the scrappy bar-hopping district change once again, in a transition very much dictated by an influx of tech-dominant wealth.

LA HOLLY

2500 E 6th Street
Austin, TX 78702

After losing his banking job during the financial crisis of 2008, Simon Madera decided to switch tracks. He used a student loan to open Triangle Wine & Spirits, a boutique liquor store, while he was still getting his MBA at St. Edward's University. Then a transformative trip to South America opened his eyes to a calling in hospitality. He returned to open his first venture, a neighborhood bar on Burnet Road. His research led him to Linda Steele, the owner of an iconic 1970s-era Austin bar called Taco Flats, which had closed in 1981.

Madera decided to revive the institution, with Steele's blessings, and opened Taco Flats in a new location on Burnet Road. He entertained the idea of expanding the concept to East Austin, and had his eyes open for property. But when he found himself sharing drinks with friends in a little 1930s bungalow-turned-Tejano-dive-bar called Kellee's Place, he knew he'd found his next project: a tribute to the quaint, residential East Austin of yesteryear.

"The property was not really for sale, but kind of was for the right buyer," remembers Madera. "I thought the property was perfect for what would be a preservation project: La Holly, the bar of the Holly neighborhood. I reached out to [owner] Joe Perez a couple of months later about my intention to buy the property. We bonded, probably because we are both Mexican."

Madera took over the bar in 2017, initially continuing to run it as Kellee's Place while landscape designer Mark Word helped him create a welcoming backyard green space with plenty of picnic tables, shade sails, and mister fans. A Taco Flats food trailer in the backyard offers favorites like fish al pastor, choriqueso and veggie-friendly options like El Hippie, made with grilled jack cheese, refried black beans, guacamole, grilled onion, and house escabeche, all served on Madera's mom's homemade tortillas.

Before launching as La Holly in 2018, Madera completed a light remodel of the interior, revealing the home's original wood walls and installing bar tables, stools, and flat-screen TVs to show games. The exterior of the bungalow got a coat of dark grey paint and a mural by Michoacán artist Curiot, who represents mythical

Mexican legends and symbols using vivid colors and sacred geometry. Kellee's was a beer-only bar, so Madera secured a liquor license and built up a collection of over 300 bottles of agave spirits like mezcal, tequila, sotol, and bacanora. In addition to a list of ten agave cocktails, there are always two frozens available—a spicy margarita and a hibiscus mezcal drink, perfect for sipping in Austin's nearly year-round sunshine.

"Honestly, not sure how much I want to tell people about this local gem," says Madera. "It's a lot of what's right with Austin. It's very old Austin while meeting the expectations of new Austin. We do what we do, not what the press or people want us to do."

Since opening La Holly, Madera has continued to take on preservation projects. Carne Lenta, a barbecue version of Taco Flats, is located in a 1940s garage in Smithville, about an hour east of Austin, and Hooper's is a Southern restaurant in a historic Victorian home in Kingsland that was part of the original Texas Chainsaw Massacre movie set.

"To me, buildings with a history are exciting because it gives me the opportunity to connect the old with the new through a restaurant and bar," says Madera. "I think it's much easier to build from scratch or find built-to-suit type buildings, but that feels more about the dollar and less about the charm and soul of a city, town, building, or neighborhood. I've taken this approach because these locations have found me and I have seen them for more than just a business."

HI HAT PUBLIC HOUSE

2121 E 6th Street
Austin, TX 78702

After working as a professional drummer for his entire life, Steve Schrader decided he wanted to embark on a new adventure in his fifties. He and his wife Rena hatched a plan to open a neighborhood bar and restaurant with live music, inspired by the pubs in his home state of Wisconsin.

"They were all little narrow bars and everyone came in and knew each other," describes Schrader. "Occasionally there'd be a deer on the wall or music playing. When I was 18, I was already playing in bars out there, so that kind of influenced what I wanted to do. Plus, I've always had a love for beer, and craft beer was really taking off in 2012 when we opened up."

Schrader's service industry experience was limited to flipping burgers in high school and college, so he gained some kitchen experience working as a prep cook for a friend, where he also connected with the chef and sous chef who have now been with him for 9 years. They secured an unassuming space in the corner of a building on East 6th Street and Robert T Martinez Jr. Boulevard, and that has been their home for the last decade—including the year and a half they were forced to close and renovate after pipes burst during Austin's infamous ice storm in February 2021.

"The ceiling gave in and every piece of equipment was ruined," remembers Schrader. "There were icicles on the inside of the building, water dripping from every light fixture, and three inches of water on the floor."

Though the rebuild was challenging to say the least, it presented the Schraders with the opportunity to make both cosmetic and functional improvements. They replaced all their furniture, opting for lower tables and chairs in lieu of the original bar tables and stools, and opening up the view to the corner stage, where there's almost always live music with no cover. The wooden slats across the new bar act like an acoustic barrier, improving the sound. And new yellow and red patterned wallpaper adds a vibrant pop of color and energy to the space, which features hi hat cymbals hanging from the ceiling, a box-shaped cajón by the red-curtained stage, and a timpani fashioned into a draft beer system.

Hi Hat had previously only served beer, but the Schraders used their unplanned break to secure a liquor license, then relaunched with a full bar and specialty cocktails. And despite their robust food program, they'd incredulously been working with just several electric burners and an oven. They upgraded to a flat top and gas burners during the rebuild, and now the food program is better than ever. Chef Thomas Reeh creates upscale pub food using high quality ingredients from local purveyors like Windy Hill Ranch and 44 Farms. Highlights include their exception bar burger, and the "Daily Bread," which is a toast dish with toppings that rotate weekly, from garlic-herb escargot to tomato confit calamari to a pozole-themed composition made with goat, hominy, hatch green chilis, and cabbage.

Bar manager Paige Ervin similarly stocks the bar with as many local products as possible: Nine Banded whiskey, Deep Eddy Vodka, Still Austin gin and whiskey, beer from (512) Brewing, Zilker Brewing Company, Independence Brewing Co., Hops and Grain, Meanwhile Beer, Austin Beerworks, St. Elmo Brewing Company, and more. Each Sunday from 1 to 3pm, guests can enjoy live jazz alongside Hi Hat's incredible Bloody Mary, made with a mix of "yum yums"—finely chopped olives, garlic, radishes, jalapeños, and carrots—and smoked paprika celery salt. On Turntable Tuesday, locals bring in their own vinyl to play. Wine bottles dip to half price on Wine Wednesdays, and Thursday brings pint nights and burger specials.

"We'll get kiddos and families in for dinner," says Ervin. "We'll get solo bar dudes who are into beer or trying to pick up ladies. We get young couples that live in the neighborhood and musicians on their way to rehearsal or coming here after playing at the jazz club down the street. We're very much a neighborhood Cheers bar—it's a mix of everyone!"

REPOSADO OLD FASHIONED

Most of the Hi Hat staff loves tequila, so their work gatherings typically involve margaritas. Bar manager Paige Ervin wanted to create a sipper tequila cocktail with less acidity — more of a nightcap to better highlight the flavor of the tequila. She chose reposado because of its notes of vanilla, jasmine, and citrus. A few dashes of orange bitters bring out the aromatic and citrus elements of the spirits.

2 oz. reposado tequila

3 dashes Angostura aromatic bitters

2 dashes Angostura orange bitters

¼ to ½ oz. simple syrup, depending on sweetness preference

Orange peel

Luxardo cherry, to garnish

1. Add the tequila, bitters, and simple syrup to a mixing glass.
2. Add enough ice to break just above the liquid line. Stir gently around edges for 15-20 seconds.
3. Add a large ice cube (2-inch cube if possible but any large whiskey rock will do) to a rocks glass and pour the mixture down the inside of the glass to avoid "breaking" the ice.
4. Express orange peel over the glass and run along the inside before dropping on top of the ice. Skewer a cherry and lay across the glass.

WHISLER'S & MEZCALERÍA TOBALÁ

1816 E 6th Street
Austin, TX 78702

I remember the days when Whisler's felt like a beautiful, well-kept secret. That time is long gone— in fact, it's hard to snag a seat here, especially on weekends— but amazingly, they've managed to maintain the same provocative vibe while serving exquisite cocktails, even with the high volume they're serving. And that is a true feat.

The old stone building on the corner of East 6th and Chicon was originally a grain mill built in 1917, and then a pizza joint before it became Rabbit's Lounge, a local watering hole owned by Rosalio "Rabbit" Duran, who turned the space into a haven for Chicano politicians, hosted community fundraisers and hired at-risk youth, teaching them to barback and bartend. After 40 years of running Rabbit's, Duran decided to retire and lease the space in 2013 to Scranton Twohey, who had been managing Rainey Street's busy Clive Bar for years before deciding to break out on his own project.

Twohey began to peel away the layers on the building, exposing the stone walls of the interior, then filling the space with antique furniture and decor he'd been collecting at estate sales and flea markets. The mirror behind the back bar came from an antique French Murphy bed, the bar seats are covered in old canvas postal bags, and a burnished old bathtub on the patio provides endless photo opps. The entire place is covered in a thick, intentional layer of patina and illuminated by flickering candlelight, which adds to the intrigue of it all. Even the name Whisler's was born from a sign Twohey scavenged at a market, which now hangs behind the bar.

"We create a vibe," says general manager Matt Wenger. "What Scranton has done such a great job in doing is making sure every one of your senses is hit when you walk through the door: the smell of palo santo, the sight and taste of the cocktails, the ambiance of the inside bar, only being candlelit, making sure we have real glassware. All the little things we could have sacrificed because we're so busy."

On a typical Saturday, Whisler's will serve between 3 and 4,000 guests, and they sell roughly 100,000 Old Fashioneds a year— yet the cocktails remain as intricate and well-made as ever. They're one of the few bars in town crafting large format ice in house. The menu

DRINK LIKE A LOCAL: AUSTIN

changes four times a year, and the team spends a month and a half perfecting each drink before releasing it.

On the building's exterior, there is a staircase leading to a door upstairs. On Thursday through Saturday, you can choose from over 300 bottles of mezcal and other agave spirits at Mezcalería Tobalá, served in traditional clay copitas with slices of orange and sal de gusano set-ups. Twohey's friends at Illegal Mezcal helped him design the space, which truly feels like you're stepping into a rustic bar in a little Oaxacan puebla, with its exposed stone walls, antique ceiling tiles, flickering veladoras, and a huapango- and cumbia-dominant soundtrack. You'll also find truly unique mezcal here because Whisler's collaborates with Oaxacan producers, like Gusto Histórico and Real Minero, on experimental batches bottled just for them.

Luckily, there's also delicious food available to help you soak up all the alcohol. The Golden Tiger trailer serves flavor-packed crispy chicken sandwiches, burgers, and loaded fries seven days a week. The bar celebrates occasions with free pig roasts and community crawfish boils. You might even find yourself with a cocktail in hand when a mariachi band walks through the space playing, or when the lights dim inside for a burlesque dancer to hop up on the bar for a seemingly impromptu performance.

"That's another reason this place is so exciting and just keeps getting busier," says Wenger. "It's the one place where you're not quite sure what's going to happen. The drinks tell a story and the buildings tell a story. You can come here to get hyper or be romantic or sing or shout."

LA LLORONA

Sean Skvarka, who has worked at Whisler's for over a decade, is responsible for some of the bar's most popular drinks. The legend of La Llorona is told throughout Mexico, Central, and South America, but its earliest documentation is traced back to Mexico City in the 1500s. There are varying versions of the story, but La Llorona is typically said to be the spirit of a woman that died of sorrow, or killed herself, after drowning her children when their father abandoned them. Families traditionally place wooden crosses above their doors to ward off the spirit, who is said to roam in a white dress wailing at night.

1½ oz. Hibiscus Mezcal

1 oz. Blackberry Syrup

¾ oz. fresh lemon juice

½ oz. blood orange puree

2 dashes Pepper Tincture

Blackberry, to garnish

Tajín, to garnish

1. Combine all ingredients in a shaker with ice and shake until chilled.

2. Rim a rocks glass with Tajín and fill with fresh cubes.

3. Pour over ice and garnish with a blackberry.

Hibiscus Mezcal: Combine 6 liters of mezcal, 24 hibiscus tea bags, and 10 crushed cinnamon sticks. The Whisler's team processes, using a sous vide machine, for 45 minutes at 145°F, but you can also simmer the ingredients in a pot on the stovetop too, without letting them come to a boil. Fine strain and cool before using.

Blackberry Syrup: Combine 2 pounds fresh blackberries, 3 pounds sugar, 2 pounds water and 1 oz. vodka in a Cambro or similar food storage container. Muddle and crush the blackberries and let the solution sit overnight before mashing it with a potato masher through a strainer.

Pepper Tincture: Combine 1 liter 190 proof grain alcohol, 10 sliced jalapeños, 5 sliced serranos, and 5 sliced habaneros. Let sit for at least 5 days. Peppers do not need to be strained out before use.

THE GRACKLE

1700 E 6th Street
Austin, TX 78702

You could call The Grackle a dive bar, but owner Tim Murphy might not agree with you.

"That's the real headscratcher for me— what people call a dive — because I've been to real dives and you don't necessarily feel safe in them," says Murphy, who's been working in the service industry since he was 16 years old and modeled The Grackle after the Midwestern watering holes he grew up around.

And he wants to make sure everyone feels safe at The Grackle. In fact, when the doorperson checks your card at the front door, you'll find a chalk drawing of a grackle, Austin's ubiquitous, crumb-scavenging black bird, on a branch, looking up toward a rainbow. The sign clearly states, "NO: Sexism, Racism, Homophobia, Transphobia, Xenophobia or Any General Hatefulness."

"That's always been my philosophy and it always kinda went unsaid and very rarely did we need to have a hard talk with anybody," says Murphy. "But then we elected a giant asshole for president and people started outright acting like assholes. So this is who we've always been, but we felt like we had to now paint a big picture to let you know what's not fucking tolerated...if you intend on being a dick, don't come in here. This is a place where any person should be able to find community and decent people to hang out with."

Walk inside and The Grackle embraces you in its darkness, thanks to a black ceiling and deep purple walls lit only by the glow of the jukebox, neon beer signs, illuminated dart boards, and the green billiard lamp over the pool table. The floor is mottled with an unintentional cow print where black flooring is peeling away to reveal concrete underneath. This stand-alone building was originally a house built in the late 1930s, but has been operating as a bar since the late 1970s. It was a Tejano bar called Primo's when Murphy took over and completed a quick week rehab of the space with the help of bartenders and friends before opening as The Grackle in January 2010.

"A lot of what I think people call dive bars are actually neighborhood bars," says Murphy. "And what you need to have a neighborhood bar is community. Even though we've had the majority of our neighborhood taken away —in a city that's been constantly, rapidly changing for the past 15 years, with short term Airbnb rentals replacing actual residents—we've maintained the same identity since we've opened the doors, aside from a few cosmetic changes and updates."

During the pandemic, Murphy renovated the bathrooms, installed a starburst of wood paneling behind the pool table and built wooden banquettes with slanted backs. The two black tufted leather armchairs and birdcage lamp he scored at a garage sale still stand at the entrance, the grackle painting and a blackbird squawking "No White Russians!" still grace the walls, and the bar's covered patio—known as "the birdcage"—still fills up with industry regulars sipping and smoking after their own shifts have ended.

Four street-facing signs hang across that patio, advertising "whiskey, whisky, whiskey and beer," in case there was any question about what to order here. Whisk(e)y is the specialty, and there's always around 200 labels from which to choose, plus another 4 to 7 single barrel selections. Ask for the binder and browse pages of bourbon, American single malts, rye, blended Scotch, and single malt scotch. They also boast one of the largest Japanese whisky collections in town, plus expressions from India, France, Mexico, and beyond—all available as generously-priced 2 ounce pours. "I'm not trying to run a museum—more of a library," says Murphy. "Don't just stare at it on the wall—check something out!"

Those in the know also order the Bloody Mary, which isn't advertised in any way, made with your choice of spirit, a splash of dry stout and house-made spicy pickled carrots and garlic-dill cucumbers.

For years, the bar hosted vegan trailers but it is now home to Asador Tacos, which serves award-winning street tacos, from barbacoa and carnitas to mushroom mole and cauliflower. Or order a crunchy, craveable chicken sandwich from across the street at Spicy Boys. They'll message you when it's ready, and you can enjoy your food while playing a game of tabletop Ms. Pacman or zoning out to whatever cult movie might be screening behind the bar or on the patio—if it's during South by Southwest, Apocalypse Now plays on repeat, in a twisted but beloved industry tradition. Right after Yellow Jacket (page 141), The Grackle is one of the earliest bars to open on East 6th Street, with daily hours of noon to 2 a.m. While the weekends tend to fill up with visitors staying in the area, locals still rule during the day shift.

"People don't really have parlors in their houses anymore, but that's the kind of environment I've always wanted in a bar, where you can walk in any time of day and know at least one—or five or six—people," Murphy describes. "It's almost like a block party, or going out to the fence to talk to the neighbors."

MILDRED'S BOURBON SOUR

"I had the great fortune and misfortune of growing up in a large, Irish Catholic, heavy-drinking family and, by the time I was about 7 or 8 years old, I'd been press-ganged into being my grandparents' bartender," Tim Murphy recalls. "My grandmother drank whiskey sours and my grandfather drank Old Fashioneds so by the time I was ten, I knew exactly how they liked their drinks." This is the slightly more elevated version.

1 turbinado sugar

1 dash Angostura bitters

1 splash of water

2 oz. Jim Beam

¼ lime

¼ lemon

1. Add sugar cube to the cocktail shaker with the bitters and a splash of water.

2. Muddle the cube and pour the Jim Beam over the muddler to knock loose any sugar.

3. Squeeze in citrus quarters and add a scoop of crushed ice.

4. Shake to hell to get a real nice slurry going.

5. Pour into a rocks glass ("Grandma wouldn't use fresh ice and neither do we," says Murphy) and enjoy.

YELLOW JACKET SOCIAL CLUB

1704 E 5th Street
Austin, TX 78702

In my early Austin days, I was devastated to learn that my favorite coffee shop at the time, Café Mundi, was set to close. This was 2010, mind you... I had no idea what massive changes were yet to come in this city. I also didn't know yet that the bar replacing it would become my second home for a period of time.

Yellow Jacket Social Club is a collaboration between five friends—Mimi Buscemi, Amy Mullins, Shannon LeBoeuf, Gayle Braecklein and Stan Rose—who saw a need on the eastside for a dog-friendly bar with good, simple food and cold, cheap beer.

"We always wanted a social club—something that is hyper-inclusive for the whole community," explains Buscemi, a former aesthetician. "Yellow Jackets are the [Cleburne, Texas] high school mascot of owner Stan Rose. And inspiration came from our back porches with lots of good friends coming and going, and lots of dogs."

The unique L-shaped building, set on a quiet strip of East 5th Street, is owned by the same family who owns Tamale House East next door, and its rustic, vine-covered aggregate exterior is the perfect match for the grove of crepe myrtles shading the sprawling patio, which light up with string lights at night. "We swore an oath to take extreme care and nurture and protect them," says Buscemi.

Cement sculptures, also carried over from the Café Mundi days, can be found tucked among the trees and well-seasoned picnic tables. The partners completed the built-out themselves with help from friends, like Adam Young from Old Crow Custom Works, who helped them design and build the bar and tables. The outside fence is a combination of a few torn down vert skate ramps, and much of the artwork plastering the walls inside, including hand-painted skate decks, came from members of Austin's O.G. skateboard scene who frequent the bar. Even the graffitied bathroom, with its layers upon layers of colored scribbles, is a work of art.

Basically, YJ, as it's known to regulars, is a dive bar with good taste. You can always get a $4 Coors, but there's also a seasonal cocktail menu and constantly rotating frozen drinks. The menu, which they've continued to grow and evolve through the years, goes above and beyond typical bar food— and most items are under $10. And since the bar is open every day from 11am to 2am, that makes it one of the most reliable places in the neighborhood to find both lunch, dinner, and late-night food. Choose from items like a mezze platter with warm pita, Frito pie topped with ropa vieja, and a roasted beet sandwich with chevre, arugula, and Moroccan carrots. The weekend brunch is also one of the most reasonable in town, featuring shrimp and grits, cognac date custard French toast, and an award-winning Bloody Mary.

"A good wine list was also something missing from a dive bar, so it was important to have that, too," says Buscemi. Braecklein, a former wine importer, is the partner who made that dream a reality, bringing in mostly small production, minimal intervention pro-ducers. And each week, all bottles drop to half price for Wine Wednesday.

True to the "social club" part of their name, there is always something going on at YJ: swap meets, art shows, DJs, metal shows, indie wrestling, vintage van meetups, pet adoption events. They host an annual orphan Thanksgiving feast, and I've found myself there singing karaoke on Christmas and nuzzling baby animals in an Easter Sunday petting zoo. As neighboring condos continue to rise, seek shelter in this magical grove where the crepe myrtles pipe Motörhead and everything still feels like Austin.

THE WHITE HORSE

500 Comal Street
Austin, TX 78702

The White Horse is one of those places it's hard to leave without someone buying you a shot of whiskey. Maybe the stranger sidled up at the bar next to you orders an extra and insists you take it while you're closing out, or a handful of Bandidos playing pool beckon you to join them in a toast. Both of these things have happened to me, which tells you all you need to know about this eastside honky-tonk. All kinds of people have fun here, and they want to share that fun. It's no wonder Vice magazine declared "only assholes have a bad time here."

Outside of the amazing live music, one of my favorite things about this bar is its diversity—and this has been true since it opened in December 2011. I've referred my fair share of out-of-towners here, for good reason, and it's unsurprisingly become a destination for birthday and bachelorette gatherings. But the dance floor also manages to attract a healthy mix of cowboys and bikers, hipsters and tech bros, octogenarians and undergrads. As for the drinks? The name of the game here is cheap beer and whiskey shots. Maybe a whiskey and soda, if you're feeling fancy. There's Maker's Mark on tap here, and it flows like water.

"White Horse is a honky tonk for everyone," says

co-owner Nathan Hill. "It's unapologetically Austin, Texas. You can love country music and have some killer two-step skills, or you can just be someone looking for a lively room full of all walks of life."

Hill first befriended his partner Denis O'Donnell while working at Kirby Lane Café back when it was still a 24-hour diner, then left to bartend at Hole in the Wall (page 64), another Austin icon, and hired O'Donnell on as a bartender and a booker.

"I think Hole in the Wall solidified for us what kind of space we could really thrive in," remembers Hill. "When we first walked into La Trampa [in the building now housing White Horse] we knew immediately that was the space we wanted. The area was still pretty rough, and the eastside becoming what it is now was unfathomable, so it took us another year or two to find someone willing to fund it."

That someone ended up being Marshall Mchone, who would come to Hole in the Wall each Friday to watch his daughter play. When the three put their heads together, they ended up opening a honky-tonk at a time when there were very few left in the state—and the ones that remained were booked solid with weekly residencies.

The White Horse immediately started booking favorite local acts like Croy and the Boys, Mike and the Moonpies, Leo Rondeau, and Clyde & Clem's Whiskey Business. Live music seven days a week—and three show slots each night—also offers plenty of opportunities for Hill and O'Donnell to showcase new talent in Texas swing, cosmic country, bluesy Americana, rowdy cowpunk, and other pedal steel-laced multi-hyphenate genres. Thursday through Saturday, free two-step lessons begin at 7 p.m., so you can learn the basics and immediately put them to work when the first band starts at 8 p.m.

All the acts play against ruby red velvet curtains illuminated by twinkling lights. The ceiling panels are painted dark, with a few vintage lamps lighting the dance floor, a checkered vinyl surface layered with enough grit to give it good grip for twirling. A sign with retro bulbs forming the shape of an arrow glows on the side of the stage and an identical one outside points toward the fenced-in patio, where the long-running Bomb Tacos trailer serves tacos, nachos, sandwiches, and quesadillas.

As for the bar's name, I always assumed it was a reference to that Laid Back dance floor anthem from the 1980s, but it turns out that is not the case.

"White Horse was named by Denis, who's got a touch of the metaphysical in him," explains Hill. "It actually came from a tarot card called The Chariot, where the white horse represents the pull towards good. We wanted to come in as the good guys who welcomed everyone into our home." And since even the most welcoming homes have rules, Hill adds, "But flip flops and line dancing will not be tolerated."

LA PERLA

1512 E 6th Street
Austin, TX 78702

East 6th Street was once lined with Tejano bars: Rio Rita, Club Oriente, La India Bonita, El Sapo Verde, Iron Gate Lounge, Club Primo's. One by one they changed ownership as gentrification reshaped the neighborhood, and now just one of those original bars still stands: La Perla. This 1935 house first became a bar in the early 1960s. Alberto and Nina Costilla took over La Perla in 1973 and then bought the building in 1990. Their son Eddie Costilla grew up in the bar and now runs operations.

"It's pretty much the same except for HDTV and cell phones and the digital jukebox—everything else is the same," says Costilla. "Some of our customers used to watch me when my parents were working. They'd keep an eye on me and shoot pool with me just to keep me busy."

The room on the west side of the house is occupied almost entirely by the pool table, which is occasionally draped with a tablecloth and turned into a buffet for parties, often with Costilla acting as DJ. The rest of the time, the glowing jukebox to the left of the entrance provides the soundtrack: a mix of Tejano, country, cumbia, mariachi, ranchera, and Latino pop. The music is always turned up loud enough to hear while sitting outside at their picnic tables, where you can enjoy tacos, tortas, and quesadillas served from Taqueria Doña Juanita's bright yellow trailer.

The bar itself occupies the east-facing room, and the small space is layered with relics: vintage beer ads, baseball caps and trophies, San Antonio Spurs and Atlanta Braves memorabilia, signs with lines like "In God We Trust: All Others Pay Cash" and "My Wife Has a Drinking Problem: Me!" A vintage Budweiser Clydesdale carousel and several piñatas hang from the popcorn ceiling and dollar bills are taped to each blade of the ceiling fan. A shelf in the corner, above the ATM, has been transformed into an altar with religious icons, veladora candles, and prayer cards. There's also an armadillo centerpiece offering a bucket full of koozies and a Modelo can-armadillo art piece hanging above the bar, commemorating La Perla's signature drink, the Armodelo, a Modelo Especial dressed with fresh lime juice, salt, and Tabasco sauce.

"One day we had a guy who came in hungover and asked for a Michelada," says Costilla. "I told him we

didn't have all the ingredients for it, and he asked what he could make that was close to it. I first made it in a cup but it wasn't consistent, so I started creasing the top of the can and using the top as a measuring cup."

The bar went from selling two cases of Modelo a week to ripping through 20 or 25 cases in the same time. News of the Armodelo made it up to corporate, and when they compiled a book of cocktails made with Modelo, La Perla's simple three-ingredient creation was placed right in the centerfold. Their distributor also designed a customized Armodelo neon sign, with a yellow outline of the nine-banded creature behind a Modelo can, which now hangs above the register.

A chalkboard behind the bar lists all the beer, cider, and seltzer options available, which range from $3 to $5. To survive on this street as just a beer bar these days is quite a feat, and Costilla says he has considered securing a liquor license to offer shot-and-beer specials and frozen margaritas. Of course, the building is more than old enough to be protected by historical preservation too.

"But you've got to tell them what happens in La Perla in order to be considered historic," says Costilla with a smile, "and we never tell anyone what happens here."

LOW DOWN LOUNGE

1412 E 6th Street, #3304
Austin, TX 78702

The ink had barely dried on the paperwork for Allen Demling's first bar venture when the pandemic struck. Demling had been working as a mechanical engineer for National Instruments for 15 years when he was part of a mass lay-off. Armed with a severance package and a lot of free time, he began toying with the idea of opening a bar. When he heard that the owners of The Brixton, on the corner of East 6th and Onion Street, was entertaining offers, he partnered with Tyler and Emily Brooke Van Aken—who are also partners in Shangri-La, Liberty, and Grackle, all located on East 6th Street—to open Low Down Lounge.

They gave the punk dive bar a face lift, incorporating pops of bright pink, orange, and yellow all throughout the space—most notably in the 1970s-inspired stripes running across the wall and in the vinyl chair seats. They added a pool table, with a bright yellow felt top, and spruced up the patio with an ivy wall, plants, and a photobooth. They were getting ready to open just in time for South by Southwest when the city went into lockdown. So they did what anyone would do, and started hosting various pop-ups—which involved delivering hot dogs by air cannon and burgers by zipline. Meanwhile, the Van Akens brought in managers from their other bars to train Demling on the ins and outs of management.

"They helped bring me up to speed and figure out what I needed to do to make the place run smoothly," Demling recalls. "It was interesting because they were teaching me all that during a pandemic. We literally set up a folding table and we were just selling to-go beers and frozens out of the door, and they'd show me how to do the orders, make a par sheet for inventory, list duties for bartenders and all that stuff."

While the bar industry may be new to Demling, diving headfirst into new adventures is not. As one of the founding members of the Austin Facial Hair Club, Demling—who sports an exceptionally long red beard and mustache—has traveled around the world competing in beard and mustache competitions, and appeared in a reality show called Whisker Wars. In 2008, he ran for city council, running a campaign focused on preserving the city's vibrant culture over catering to developers and corporate interests. The Low Down Lounge is an extension of his vision for the city.

"One of our goals is to try to maintain a reasonably priced bar in this area, as things get more expensive," says Demling. The tropical-leaning menu features cocktails under $10—unheard of on East 6th Street—including a large-format, flame-lit scorpion bowl for just $18. They also feature an everyday happy hour with $3 wells and $2 pints of Coors. And for just $6, you can get a RoboCop, a spin on a drink Demling's friend created in high school by turning a clipped-open Capri Sun upside down into a Smirnoff Ice… on ice—except this one subs Texas Cool, a locally made watermelon-cucumber hard seltzer, for the Smirnoff.

If the customer coloring book pages plastered on the fridge behind the bar are any indication, Low Down Lounge is a place to leave your worries at the door and embrace your inner child. Handmade tables fold down to make way for a DJ booth because dance parties break out that regularly here. On Monday nights, the assistant GM Jeannette sets up a Nintendo switch and patrons cluster together to play games like Sorry, Trouble, and Battleship.

"We try to just come up with goofy ideas," says Demling. We've done punk rock prom. For Bosses Day, we celebrated Bruce Springsteen, the only real boss we care about. Our holiday party was Star Wars-themed. We just like to come up with things that aren't what everyone else is doing. It makes it a lot more fun for us too."

More Locally Loved East 6th Street Bars & Breweries:

MAMA DEAREST
515 Pedernales Street, Austin, TX 78702

ZILKER BREWING COMPANY AND TAPROOM
1701 E 6th Street, Austin, TX 78702

LAZARUS BREWING CO.
1902 E 6th Street, Austin, TX 78702

DAY DREAMER
1708 E 6th Street, Austin TX 78702

THE LIBERTY
1618 E 6th Street, Austin, TX 78702

DOMO ALLEY-GATO TATSU-YA
1600 E 6th Street B, Austin, TX 78702

HOTEL VEGAS
1502 E 6th Street, Austin, TX 78702

THE VOLSTEAD LOUNGE
1500 E 6th Street, Austin, TX 78702

REVELRY KITCHEN + BAR
1410 E 6th Street, Austin, TX 78702

LOLO
1504 E 6th Street, Austin, TX 78702

MILONGA ROOM
1201 E 6th Street, Austin, TX 78702

UPTOWN SPORTS CLUB
1200 E 6th Street, Austin, TX 78702

VIOLET CROWN SOCIAL CLUB
1111 E 6th Street, Austin, TX 78702

SHANGRI-LA & THE TREASURY
1016 E 6th Street, Austin, TX 78702

"DIRTY" 6TH STREET AND WEST 6TH STREET

The section of 6th Street now known as "Dirty 6th" runs from Congress Avenue to I-35, and there may not be another part of Austin that has undergone such consistent change since the city was founded. Case in point: The Ritz Theater, which opened on 6th Street in 1929, has been a movie theater, porn theater, live music venue, biker bar, pool hall, and a location of an Alamo Drafthouse before transitioning to its current state as a comedy club owned by Joe Rogan.

Originally named Pecan Street, the historic avenue appeared in the first maps of Austin as early as 1839. Pecan Street served as Austin's commercial hub, particularly after the arrival of the railroad in 1871. The beautiful Victorian storefronts lining 6th Street now were some of the city's first buildings, housing offices, warehouses, and showrooms for railroad-dependent enterprises, plus dry good stores, saloons, blacksmiths, tailors, and boarding houses. And while the rest of Austin was segregated under Jim Crow, 6th Street remained open to all, so many of these businesses were run by Black, Lebanese, Latino, Jewish, and Chinese entrepreneurs. As Congress Avenue began to take over as the more fashionable shopping district, many of 6th Street's businesses moved or shut down.

A post-World War II economic slump sent the thoroughfare into further decline and it started to become more known for its seedy bar scene. By the late 1960s, it was the city's red light district.

In the 1970s, Dirty 6th started to see a revival as it took its form as the Live Music Capital. The legendary club Antone's opened in 1975, giving a stage to the city's many talented blues musicians before attracting touring artists. Esther's Follies, which still puts on shows every weekend, opened its vaudeville theater on the corner of Red River and 6th. By the 1980s, The Black Cat Lounge began its 17-year run hosting a spectrum of bands, from rock to blues to country to jam bands. In its musical heyday, Dirty 6th was lined with live music venues: Steamboat, Cannibal Club, Bates Motel, Headliners East, The White Rabbit. You could see blues at Joe's Generic, then catch reggae at Flamingo Cantina, and a punk show at the first Austin location of Emo's, all within the span of a few blocks. But as larger venues started opening around town, drawing in touring acts, these small venues started rapidly losing revenue and shut down one by one, with the exception of Flamingo Cantina, which is still going strong, and Antone's, which has changed ownership and moved several times, but now resides on 5th Street. The younger crowds that began frequenting Dirty 6th cared more about drinking on the cheap and milling around on the street, which gets shut down to traffic on the weekends. To this day, those beautiful historic buildings are home to shot bars, the occasional tattoo shop, frat boys on mechanical bulls, and door guys hawking dollar drinks. Once you cross West 6th Street, the clientele becomes a bit older and the bars more expensive. Throngs of recent grads and young professionals fill rooftops and patios, and many of the bars start to take on a clubbier vibe, with (often indiscriminate) dress codes enforced.

That being said, there are still some gems on this street; you've just got to dig for them a little. The bar inside the Driskill Hotel, the city's oldest operating hotel, is like a step back in time, when politicians mingled with cattle barons. Punk dive bar Casino El Camino (page 158) is an institution that's not to be missed, and serves their famous burgers until last call. Mala Vida and Vaquero Taquero are breathing new life back into 6th Street, and drawing a young Latinx crowd back downtown for dancing and late-night tacos. Upscale restaurant Parkside and its sister restaurant, Backspace Pizza, are putting out some of the best food on 6th Street, and Midnight Cowboy (page 161) is a speakeasy serving cocktails out of a former brothel, and one of my favorite spots to ponder the wild history of the city center.

CASINO EL CAMINO

517 E 6th Street
Austin, TX 78701

A step into Casino El Camino is like a glimpse into the Dirty 6th Street of yesteryear, when the strip was a destination for sold-out punk shows at Emo's, The Ritz, and The Black Cat Lounge; they are all now shuttered. In 1990, after attending the fourth South by Southwest, punk rocker Paul Eighmey—whose nom de guerre has been "Casino" for the past 40 years—moved with his band to Austin from Buffalo. When they broke up shortly after the move, he decided to open a bar.

The Victorian limestone building where he set up shop was built in the 1880s by Lebanese immigrants as a general store with a residence upstairs. The building went on to become a hardware store, shoe store, pawn shop, barbecue joint, and fetish shop before it became Casino El Camino in 1994. The ghost of a child that died in the upstairs room is said to haunt the space, and they even keep a plush animal in the corner, with a plaque explaining it, for "Mary."

Back in 1994, downtown had a "funky and edgy live music scene with a sense of community," remembers Casino, and his bar certainly became a stalwart piece of the puzzle. And though the neighborhood has changed plenty, Casino remains virtually the same as the day it opened. "The bar has changed very little," says Casino.

"Regulars come and go. CDs get changed out on the jukebox. Prices increase. If it ain't broke, don't fuck with it."

The jukebox, which consistently wins an award from the Austin-American Statesman, is a music nerd's dream, with over 100 albums spanning Black Sabbath to the likes of Buck Owens, Nancy Sinatra, and Gang of Four. The movie screen is usually playing a cult or campy film by directors such as Russ Meyer or Frank Henenlotter. And the bar's overall design pays tribute to Casino's love of punk rock, horror movies, and Meso-American archaeology with a distinct curation of framed movie posters, skulls, totems, hot-rod flames, pin-ups, and gargoyles.

For a city that loves drinking as much as Austin does, there really aren't enough options for late-night dining. Casino is my go-to downtown recommendation, serving until 1:30am seven days a week. They also open at 11:30 am every day—prime time for enjoying their Bloody Mary, which is made-to-order on a heat scale of 1 to 10, using their house tomato juice base and garnished with a garden of veggie accouterments.

Before the bar appeared on *Diners, Drive-Ins and Dives* in 2008, the bar's food menu was a bit of a best-kept-secret for those in the know. But when Guy Fieri broke the news, it became a bona fide food destination, both for locals and visitors, with the Buffalo wings, verde chili fries, and signature Angus burgers being the most popular. During peak dining hours and busy nights, the wait for one of the burgers can be up to an hour or more. Grab a PBR and settle into a game of pool on the second floor: it'll be worth the wait.

MIDNIGHT COWBOY

313 E 6th Street
Austin, TX 78701

When walking down the section of 6th Street known as "Dirty 6th," not much should come as a surprise. A contortionist may pop out of a suitcase, for instance, or you might encounter fully costumed Teenage Mutant Ninja Turtles dancing in the street. A veteran stoically holds a massive American flag on a pole, unbothered by shrieking, scantily clad bachelorettes, while a man with a microphone preaches to whoever will listen. But to find out that some of the best cocktails in the city are being made in the middle of a street filled with door guys hawking dollar shots to stumbling passersby? Now, I'd call that a surprise.

Look for the "Midnight Cowboy Modeling" sign at the top of the building; it is indeed left behind from the building's brothel days, which ended a mere decade ago. Then trace a line down to the red light glowing outside the door, where you'll ring a doorbell labeled "Harry Craddock." An attendant will slide open a little window to confirm your identity before granting you access.

Once inside, the chaos of 6th Street will seem far, far away. Black, diamond-tufted booths, dark floral wallpaper, scalloped vintage ceiling tiles, and glowing wall sconces give the narrow, mirror-lined main bar a very film noir train car feel. Larger parties can reserve one

of three private rooms in the back, where you can flip a switch—which turns on another red light—for service. And yes, these are the very same rooms where other services used to be provided in Midnight Cowboy's past life.

The expertly crafted cocktails span from riffs on classics to thoroughly innovative creations made tableside on a bar cart. Get your camera ready because each drink—and its glassware and garnish—is a work of art. You'll need to make a reservation online for a booth or room, but an outdoor patio with a simplified cocktail list is available for walk-ins too. If ever you find yourself in the belly of the beast that is Dirty 6th Street, consider this your escape plan.

PALO SANTO FLIP

This Midnight Cowboy favorite is a twist on a classic called the Lawn Tennis Cooler, which dates back to the origins of the game itself in 1891. This version adheres to the basics with brandy, ginger beer, lemon, and a whole egg, but the twist comes in the finish, as the intense flavor of Smith & Cross plays with the banana and toasted coconut notes.

1 oz. Saint Louise Brandy

½ oz. Smith & Cross Rum

¼ oz. Tempus Fugit Crème de Banane

½ oz. fresh lime juice

½ oz. fresh lemon juice

¼ oz. Toasted Coconut Demerara

1 whole egg

3 oz. ginger beer

toasted coconut and mint, to garnish

1. Combine all of the ingredients, except the ginger beer and garnishes, in a cocktail shaker with ice, shake well, and strain into a red wine glass.

2. Add the ginger beer, fresh ice, and garnish with toasted coconut and a robust mint bouquet.

Toasted Coconut Demerara: In a saucepan, combine 10 oz. Demerara sugar, 5 oz. water, and 3 tablespoons toasted shredded coconut and simmer until sugar is fully dissolved. Let cool, strain, and store.

STAR BAR

600 W 6th Street
Austin, TX 78701

Drive by Star Bar, with its many patio TVs, and you could mistake it for a common sports bar. But longtime locals know there's much more to it than that. In fact, this was the very first bar to open on West 6th Street in 1995, in a 1970s bank building—the old vault is now the bar's walk-in cooler. Originally, Star Bar was a certified dive: a carpeted, windowless space with a large, star-shaped bar.

When the original owners decided to move on to other ventures in 2008, they had a handshake agreement to sell the building to the late restaurateur Kevin Williamson. But since restaurants were his specialty, he partnered with FBR Management to refresh the building and concept. This was their very first project of this sort, before they went on to preserve a number of other iconic Austin establishments.

The bar's signature curved neon sign still serves as a

familiar beacon on the corner of 6th and Nueces. But the bar's interior was remodeled to bring in light—hello windows!—and include some more sleek textures—goodbye carpet!—while still maintaining a retro feel with round red booth seating, wood-paneled walls, and classic red pizzeria votive candles. They expanded the patio, then began adding more TVs as the demand rose; currently there are 27 sets. They also expanded their bar program, adding both craft cocktails and beer to the menu. There are now 14 constantly rotating taps pouring one of the most diverse selections of beer found on West 6th Street.

"Star Bar was on the front end of the craft beer revolution of 2010," remembers Max Moreland, who was the GM of Star Bar before he was FBR's Chief Operating Officer. "Back then, if you wanted a good beer, you had to go to a place that specialized in it. But we were one of the first to put great beer in a bar right on West 6th Street."

As the area began to blow up all around them, Star Bar maintained a cozy familiarity most sports bars lack, and continues to attract Capitol employees and lawyers who work in the neighborhood just north of the bar. Consider it the eye of the storm that is West 6th Street. "Our back patio is a little removed from the chaos, so you kind of forget that it's there," says Moreland.

The sprawling patio has also helped launch a number of successful food businesses through the years: Hat Creek Burger Company, Peached Tortilla, Valentina's Tex-Mex Barbecue, and Tumble 22, to name a few. These days, locally loved VIA 313 draws in plenty of business for its craveable, Detroit-style pies.

Just recently, Star Bar brought back a cult favorite by popular demand: its over-the-top Hail Mary, a $35 Bloody Mary loaded with everything from pizza to donuts to chunks of cheese (for all the Green Bay Packers fans who have called this bar home for the last 15 years).

THE TINIEST BAR IN TEXAS

817 W 5th Street
Austin, TX 78703

Is it really, though?

"We hope so, or we've been lying to people for 15 years," says Neal Breen, who had been bartending and managing bars for ten years before the owners of The Tiniest Bar in Texas moved to Hawaii during the pandemic and handed him the keys to run the show.

The little red building, which is just shy of 350 square feet and comically diminutive next to The Bowie apartment building towering just behind it, was originally the office for a car dealership before it became a bar in 2007. The interior has enough space for a bathroom and the bar itself. While you can step inside to order, most people do so through the window looking out onto the porch, which features a TV and some high-top tables. Down the stairs, a spacious patio offers more seating and food options from Austin's Habibi and Super Burrito food trucks.

The Tiniest Bar is proof that you don't need bells and whistles to create community. While, like most downtown bars, this one has become a popular destination for tourists and bachelorettes—thanks in part to their signature glittering Tiny Disco Ball shot—it remains just as popular with locals too. And, as the only bar on this section of West Fifth street, and close to both West 6th Street and Seaholm but somewhere between the two, it's really in a place of its own, relying more on its intentional patrons than random foot traffic. Of course, the reasonable prices on draft beers, cocktails, and boilermakers are also a draw—particularly during happy hour when wells go down to $4 and pints to $5.

"I've gotten to know a lot of our regulars, and have even spent time with many of them outside of the bar, as has much of the staff," says Breen. "I know this term is beaten to death and often false, but we really are a big family, if sometimes dysfunctional. Many people in the neighborhood come by most days to watch a game on the TV, grab a quick drink, and catch up with the bartender, or come to our holiday parties. Good people from all walks of life, and I'm very glad to have met each of them."

More Locally Loved "Dirty" 6th and West 6th Street Bars:

MALA VIDA
708 E 6th Street, Austin, TX 78701

VAQUERO TAQUERO
603 Sabine Street, Austin, TX 78701

FLAMINGO CANTINA
515 E 6th Street, Austin, TX 78701

THE JACKALOPE
404 E 6th Street, Austin, TX 78701

THE DEAD RABBIT
204 E 6th Street, Austin TX 78701

THE DRISKILL BAR
604 Brazos Street, Austin, TX 78701

THE IRON BEAR
301 W 6th Street, Austin, TX 78701

THE BEEZ KNEEZ
610 Nueces Street Suite 100, Austin, TX 78701

WIGGLE ROOM
612 Nueces Street, Austin, TX 78701

RUSTIC TAP
613 W 6th Street, Austin, TX 78701

DIRTY BILL'S
511 Rio Grande Street, Austin, TX 78701

WEST 5TH STREET, WEST END, TARRYTOWN, CLARKSVILLE, AND WEST AUSTIN

Once West 6th Street and West 5th Street cross Lamar Boulevard, they change drastically. This section of West 6th forms the southern border to Clarksville, a very affluent neighborhood located just west of downtown. The historic bungalows on this part of West 6th Street mostly house offices now, and West 5th is lined with luxury apartment buildings and mixed-use development. And yet, two historic and beloved bars—The Mean-Eyed Cat (page 179) and Donn's Depot (page 175)—continue to live on, thanks to major support from the community. A big chunk of West 6th Street has been acquired by McGuire Moorman Lambert Hospitality, which owns an empire of restaurants and bars around town, including June's All Day (page

298). On West 6th alone, they operate Sweetish Hill, Pecan Square Café, Clark's Oyster Bar, Howard's, and Rosie's Wine Bar, with more to come. Weekends are packed at Better Half Coffee & Cocktails and Hold Out Brewing, an all-day café and the neighborhood's only brewery, both opened by the owner of Little Brother (page 241) and his partners. Zoning makes it impossible for many bars to exist west of MoPac. Deep Eddy Cabaret (page 182) has been open so long they've been grandfathered in, and spots like The Beer Plant and Ski Shores Cafe are restaurants with notable bar programs. Just a half mile north of West 6th on Lamar in The West End, you can find Saints bar Shoal Creek Saloon dishing out New Orleans-inspired cuisine, get a beer at The Tavern (page 172), the city's oldest and most haunted sports pub, and access Wink's entire menu at the long-running restaurant's adjacent wine bar.

THE TAVERN

922 W 12th Street
Austin, TX 78703

The Tavern, set on the corner of West 12th Street and Lamar Boulevard, looks more like a German restaurant in Fredericksburg than Austin's oldest sports bar. This iconic half-timbered house was built in 1916 as The Enfield Grocery Store and modeled after the architecture made popular by German public houses of the time.

Once the 21st Amendment repealed the ban of alcohol in 1933, The Tavern was born. It quickly became known for its cold beer and burgers and, soon afterward, its air conditioning. It was one of the first places in Austin to have a system installed, and the iconic neon "air conditioning" sign still glows outside.

In 2018, Shannon Sedwick and Michael Shelton, owners of downtown theater Esther's Follies, purchased this piece of Austin history in order to preserve it, just as they had done to save The Velveeta Room and Stars Cafe. They kept the interior mostly the same but revamped the food menu with chef Johnny Romo, using fresh, local ingredients when possible in modernized pub fare like the barbecue-loaded Mahomes fries and a grilled chicken and veggie entree called The Wendy Davis. You can also still order classic chicken wings and queso to go with one of the rotating craft beers on tap.

Despite many renovations through the years and over 30 HD-TVs playing games at all times, this 5,000 square

foot Austin landmark still feels like it exists in a different era. The wooden interior features green molding to match the picnic tables outside. A well-worn staircase leads to the spacious second floor, and there are nooks and crannies everywhere, from booths looking out onto Lamar to high-top tables with barstools and longer tables for larger groups. Relics from the past are tucked throughout the space, from old neon signs and stained glass to an antique fortune telling machine, an out-of-commission Wurlitzer jukebox, and the popular shuffleboard table.

The Tavern is also said to be one of the most haunted places in Austin. During Prohibition, the upstairs is rumored to have become a speakeasy, casino, and brothel. And as legend has it, when a local politician was discovered visiting the illicit operation, he murdered a prostitute named Emily in retribution. Through the years, both guests and employees have heard phantom footsteps, seen TVs shut off, and drawers slam closed, or felt a pinch or tap on the arm when no one is around. Some have even reportedly seen the apparition of a woman roaming around the second floor.

True to form, thespian duo Sedwick and Shelton have written a murder mystery dinner theater experience called Haunting of the Tavern, with interactive shows at the bar. The show stars current and former Esther's Follies cast members plus other local entertainers, and each one includes a three-course meal and three acts of mystery-solving comedy, with a different ending each night.

DONN'S DEPOT

1600 W 5th Street
Austin, TX 78703

In a city where rapid growth is a sore subject, Donn's Depot is the sigh of relief we all need. This section of Fifth Street, just west of downtown, is a patchwork of luxury high-rises, architecture studios, and a Jaguar dealership. Yet this piano bar and saloon still stands, a well-worn reminder of simpler times.

In 1972, the bar's founder, Bob Ogden, purchased this 19th-century train depot for $300 and relocated it from McNeil, Texas, just north of Austin, to what was, at the time, a barren road off the Texas 1 Loop expressway. The McNeil Depot had one of the first mixed-drink licenses in Travis County, so it was immediately popular. Ogden began adding train cars to expand the bar: a big silver car forms the back wall of the club and acts as office and storage space, a boxcar became elevated seating overlooking the dancefloor, and a candy-striped caboose, complete with its original cupola, houses the women's restroom.

Pianist Donn Adelman regularly drew a crowd to the dance floor crooning covers of songs by Johnny Cash, Elvis, Roy Orbison, Frank Sinatra, Waylon Jennings, and more. So when Ogden was looking to sell the bar in 1978, Adelman took it over and it became Donn's Depot. Almost fifty years later, 83-year-old Adelman still plays with his band, Donn and the Stations Masters, every Friday night. And for the last 25 years, his son Matt

Adelman has been the house drummer, with the iconic velvet Elvis as his background.

"Some bars have a theme and they buy antiques from other places and hang them on their walls to make it look like that was their deal," says Matt. "None of that here. All of this is antique railroad memorabilia, beer signs, all kinds of shit! It's all been here for almost fifty years and most of it's older than that already. Most of it became antique just sitting here!"

The interior of Donn's is lined with signed photos from visiting musicians and patrons through the years, an antique chalkboard train schedule, tin signs for New York Central System, Union Pacific, and Missouri-Kansis-Texas Line—and a wooden Great Northern Railway sign Matt suspects is at least 100 years old like the train cars themselves. Between November and February, the place is glistening like Santa's workshop, trimmed to the nines with twinkling lights, tinsel, and snowflakes. It's especially heart-warming to see this place so filled with life after their lights went dark for so long during the pandemic.

"During COVID, someone started a GoFundMe to support Austin live music, and people just started mailing us checks and saying, 'Make sure Donn's stay alive,'" says Matt. "One day El Arroyo's sign read 'Austin isn't Austin without Donn's.' That meant so much to us."

Because of that unsolicited community support, Donn's was able to make repairs while they were closed, and then fix the subsequent broken pipes and water damage after the city suffered a record ice storm in 2021.

"All the money that people had helped us raise while we were closed is probably why we're still alive," says Matt. "It was rough for a while, but we did it thanks to the generosity of Austin and all our regulars."

These days, Donn's is as busy as ever. The same regulars who've been coming for decades sidle up to the bar when it opens and enjoy their usual drinks over Jeopardy. Amy and her fluffy white dog Louise settle into their spot. Shelly, with his signature black-rimmed glasses, cowboy hat, and "Chick Magnet" shirt, can be seen twirling ladies around the dancefloor, while Joe slips off his shoes and interprets the music in a flowy, sparkly shirt and socks. And then there's the new wave of patrons, from the fraternity types who flock here on weekends to the service industry crowd who hang here on quieter Mondays.

"Sometimes it weirds people out that you've got all generations here," says Matt. "People can be graduating from UT and they'll come sit here with their grandparents and they all have a blast. Where else do you do that?"

SIDECAR

Thanks to their loyal following of multi-generational regulars, Donn's gets a variety of requests for popular cocktails from all different periods of time. Tammi Schissler, who's been behind the bar here for 32 years, says the Sidecar is one of those. While the exact origin of the cocktail is unclear, it is thought to have been invented around the end of World War I, and the Ritz Hotel in Paris claims it as their own invention. It's basically a daiquiri, with brandy in place of rum and Cointreau acting as a sweetener rather than sugar.

1 ½ oz. cognac

¾ oz. orange liqueur (such as Cointreau)

¾ oz. fresh lemon juice

1. Add cognac, liqueur and lemon into a shaker and shake with ice until well-chilled.

2. Coat the rim of a coupe glass with sugar, then strain the cocktail into prepared glass. Garnish with an orange twist or cherry and serve.

MEAN-EYED CAT

1621 W 5th Street
Austin, TX 78703

When I moved to Austin in 2005, Mean-Eyed Cat was one of the first bars I stepped inside. As a fresh transplant from the Northeast, the little wooden bar—with its peeling paint and rusty corrugated metal—was the most Texas thing I'd ever laid eyes on.

Named after one of Johnny Cash's lesser-known songs, the bar is stenciled with his lyrics and plastered with stickers, license plates, framed photos, and album covers. Signage and saw blades serve as clues to the space's past life as a chainsaw repair shop—one that appeared in The Texas Chainsaw Massacre, in fact. The building, now over 150 years old, is thought to have originally been a church, and it housed Cut-Rite Chainsaws in the mid-20th century, until the space was converted into a bar in 2004. Not only do folks still show up with chainsaws in need of repair, but the former owner, Bill Taylor, is said to be the resident friendly ghost.

In 2013, the bar changed hands. Now run by FBR Management, they maintained Mean-Eyed's lovably rustic look despite a remodel that resulted in a spacious patio and an expanded 160-person capacity. Metcalf BBQ now serves brisket, turkey, and pulled pork plates, plus specials like Mean-Eyed Mac, shells and cheese with your choice of protein, out of a back room. These days,

a mixed-use development has bellied right up to the edge of the property, where a beautiful 400-year-old live oak tree, which they've named George, sprawls over the patio and the building. George's status as one of the oldest trees in Austin means the bar is forever safe from development under city ordinance.

"Trees like George are very protected so they were unable to build past the current root system, which is where the apartments stop," declares FBR's Chief Operating Officer Max Moreland. "Thanks to George, Mean-Eyed Cat was able to use one of its nine lives and remain. Without the tree, we would be gone!"

MEAN MARGARITA

The Mean Marg is one of Mean-Eyed Cat's signature libations. A little sweet and tart with a kick from jalapeño and habanero, this is best enjoyed on a sunny, breezy day on the West 5th Street patio.

1 orange wedge

2 jalapeño slices

2 oz. silver tequila

½ oz. orange liqueur

½ oz. Habanero Syrup

1 oz. fresh lime juice

1. Rim your drinking glass of choice with Tajín salt powder.
2. In a pint glass, muddle the orange and jalapeño slices, fill the glass with ice, add the remainder of the ingredients, shake well, and strain into the prepared glass over ice.

Habanero Syrup: Halve 2 or 3 habanero peppers, being sure to keep the seeds, and place them in a saucepan with equal parts water and sugar. Mix well and bring to a boil. Turn off the heat, let steep for 30 minutes, strain, and then cool before using.

DEEP EDDY CABARET & POOL BURGER

2315 Lake Austin Boulevard
Austin, TX 78703

Will Bridges's memories of Deep Eddy Cabaret date back to his early childhood when he passed it every day on his way to and from school. "On the way home at 3 o'clock, there'd be people milling around and the door would open and a big plume of smoke would come out and I just remember thinking, 'What are those adults doing?'"

So when he heard that the owners of Deep Eddy Cabaret were looking for someone to buy the business, he jumped at the chance to preserve this Austin institution. Fittingly, the musician had already been a partner in opening barbecue restaurant and music venue Lambert's in the historic J.P Schneider building, relaunching Willie Nelson's Arlyn Studios, revitalizing the historic blues club Antone's, and preserving Cisco's, the oldest operating Tex-Mex restaurant in Austin.

Bob Bullock was a famous regular while he was Lieutenant Governor of Texas; he would order one cold mug of beer at a time, a practice they still call "Bob Bullock style." Jimmie Dale Gilmore from The Flatlanders wrote "Deep Eddy Blues" about the bar. But the original structure was built in 1913 by Walter Johnson, first existing as a grocery store. Before Lake Austin's dam system was built, the area of the Colorado River a literal stone's throw from the site was named for a big rock that jutted out into the water, creating a natural deep eddy. This was a popular swimming hole and fishing spot, and locals would pick up their bait at the grocery store before heading down to the water. In fact, the words "groceries and minnows" can still be seen on the west side of the building.

In 1951, husband and wife Raymond and Mickey Hickman turned it into Deep Eddy Cafe, but eventually changed the name to Deep Eddy Cabaret because the beer-only bar never sold any food! (Hilariously, the bar still regularly gets calls inquiring about whether it's that kind of cabaret.) When Raymond tragically died in a motorcycle accident, Mickey threw herself into

running the bar until 1996, when her son Butch and his wife Patti took over. Deep Eddy Cabaret was more than a bar— it was their family, and that tradition continues on to this day, with regulars who have been frequenting the establishment for decades and bartenders who have been working there just as long.

"Most of the folks that come aren't coming to get loaded," says Bridges. "They come because of community— it's like their living room. We have a group we call the Gunsmoke Crew because they watch Gunsmoke re-runs every day. There used to be a Wheel of Fortune group that came in too."

When Butch and Patti were ready to retire in 2014, Bridges and his father bought Deep Eddy Cabaret, changing little about the bar outside of incorporating a POS system and obtaining a liquor license. The wood paneled walls are still plastered with photos, neon lights, and metallic beer ads, and there's just enough linoleum floor tile space in the back to navigate a game of pool, Atari, or Golden Tee. The bar also boasts one of the best jukeboxes in town, spanning Otis Redding to Muddy Waters, Roy Orbison, and The Clash.

In 2017, Bridges partnered with local restaurateur Larry McGuire to open a tiki bar called Pool Burger directly behind Deep Eddy Cabaret, where the bar's general manager historically lived. Now patrons can follow up a swim at Deep Eddy with a stacked Wagyu cheeseburger and a frozen Hurricane at Pool Burger, followed by an icy cold pitcher of Peacemaker at Deep Eddy Cabaret. A visit to all three, known as a Hippie Triathlon, is the best kind of summer training.

POOL BURGER'S MAI TAI

Some days, a mini pitcher of Mexican lager from Deep Eddy
Cabaret is all your heart desires. But other days, particularly those
sizzling summer afternoons, call for a boozy, tropical creation
from Pool Burger. This classic Mai Tai recipe is such a staple of the
tiki bar, they have it printed on the back of their commemorative
glassware.

1 oz. agricole rhum (they use Rhum J.M. 110 Proof)

1 oz. Jamaican black rum (they use Hamilton Pot Still Black)

½ oz. orange shrub (they like the brands La Favorite or Clément,
but feel free to substitute dry curaçao or another orange liqueur)

½ oz. orgeat almond syrup (they make their own, but you can also
use expressions from Giffard or Liber & Co)

1 oz. fresh lime juice

Extra lime and mint, to garnish

1. Combine all of the ingredients in a cocktail shaker with ice, shake
   well, and strain into a tiki mug over crushed ice.

2. Garnish with fresh mint and extra lime.

More Locally Loved West Austin Bars:

WINK WINE BAR
1014 N Lamar Boulevard, Austin, TX 78703

SHOAL CREEK SALOON
909 N Lamar Boulevard, Austin, TX 78703

ROSIE'S WINE BAR
1130 W 6th Street, Austin, TX 78703

HOWARD'S BAR AND CLUB
1130 W 6th Street, Austin, TX 78703

BETTER HALF COFFEE & COCKTAILS
406 Walsh Street, Austin, TX 78703

HOLD OUT BREWING
1208 W 4th Street, Austin, TX 78703

BAR PEACHED
1315 W 6th Street, Austin, TX 78703

NIGHTCAP
1401 W 6th Street, Austin, TX 78703

NEIGHBORHOOD VINTNER
3663 Bee Caves Road, #4D, Austin, TX 78746

THE BEER PLANT
3110 Windsor Road, Austin, TX 78703

FLO'S WINE BAR & BOTTLE SHOP
3111 W 35th Street, Austin, TX 78703

SKI SHORES CAFE
2905 Pearce Road, Austin, TX 78730

CAPITOL AREA AND CENTRAL CONGRESS AVENUE

While this part of the city would typically just be lumped together with the rest of "Downtown," I decided to create a section for the pocket surrounding the Texas Capitol, where iconic dive bars are juxtaposed with cocktail bars. Plus, South Congress is its own distinguishable neighborhood, so why shouldn't Central Congress Avenue—historically the city's main street—enjoy its own limelight? Much of this area directly around the Capitol is occupied by government buildings and law offices, many of them housed in Victorian homes. The lack of high-rises—thanks to the Texas Capitol View Corridors that protect the dome's obstruction—makes it feel like an older version of Austin. West of the Capitol grounds and north of the Governor's Mansion, the Texas Chili Parlor (page 190) is an absolute shanty of an institution, where you could just as easily run into a City Council Member or a celebrity. Each new graduating class of UT likes to think they discovered The Cloak

Room (page 193), another important political hub where many a handshake deal has been made.

Several blocks south of the Capitol, Here Nor There (page 202) and Small Victory (page 196) are crafting some of the best cocktails in town. In the 19th century, the central stretch of Congress south of the Capitol was known as "The Avenue," and it was Austin's most well-established business district. These days, the historic Paramount Theater is still the site of major concerts and film screenings, now joined by towering office buildings, banks, upscale retail shops, and museums, like The Mexic-Arte and The Contemporary. Live music still happens every night at Elephant Room, a basement jazz club founded in 1991, and just across the street, Mort Subite is the only bar in town specializing in Belgian beer. P6, a lounge set in a former parking garage inside The LINE Hotel, provides some of the best views of Lady Bird Lake and the South Congress bridge, especially if you can snag a sunset booking.

Colton

Elroy

St Mary's

TEXAS CHILI PARLOR

1409 Lavaca Street
Austin, TX 78701

"**W**ell, I wished I was in Austin in the Chili Parlor bar, drinking Mad Dog margaritas and not caring where you are." This Guy Clark line, which kicks off the title track to his Dublin Blues album, has drawn fans from all over the globe to seek out the Texas Chili Parlor's high-octane mezcal margarita. And if you've seen Quentin Tarantino's Death Proof, you've gotten a glimpse of the Texas Chili Parlor in this memorable scene: T. Rex plays on the jukebox while Tarantino, as the bartender, slams shots of Chartreuse—"the only liquor so good they named a color after it"—and Vanessa Ferlito gives Kurt Russell a lap dance.

Texas Chili Parlor, a little wooden shanty nestled in the shadow of the Capitol, was opened in February 1976 by Michael Wilhite and three of his friends. In 1999, when Wilhite wanted to get out of the biz, one of the bar's regulars threw his name into the hat to buy it, but the bid went to a couple instead. "He thought I was a little too crazy at the time," remembers Scott Zublin (better known as "Zoob") with a chuckle. "He might've been right." But when the new owners stopped paying taxes and the Comptroller's office padlocked the door two years later, Zoob was the first in line to save his favorite bar. At the time, Zoob was an oil drilling supervisor with

no industry experience, though he had studied hotel and restaurant management in school.

"Just short of a degree but eh... I like drinking," says Zoob with a shrug. "I came back, saved the bar on a Tuesday, we opened on Friday, I stole a chef from The Yellow Rose [an iconic Austin strip club], and we've been kickin' ass ever since."

As promised, Zoob maintained the same rustic Texan charm for which the bar was known. The all-wooden interior is a hodge-podge of street signs, beer ads, photos, and vintage neon and memorabilia. A Texas Longhorns banner drapes the door and a Lone Star flag hangs on the ceiling above the bar. A hand-painted sign lists the "rules": "No Lone Star, No Checks, No Draft, No Fries, No Foo Foo Drinks, and No Talking to Imaginary People."

The menu spans from burgers to enchiladas to fajitas, and offers six different varieties of chili, but the bean-less "bowl of red" is what you get here, in one of three different heat levels. "If you know beans about chili, you know Texas chili has no beans," says Zoob. There's even a $120 bowl of chili, which comes with a bottle of Veuve Clicquot.

The other featured drinks are notably inexpensive—most under $10. The frozen margaritas, made daily with fresh-squeezed lime juice, are strong and bright, the tongue-in-cheek Capital Cosmo is made from Bulleit Bourbon and cranberry, and the popular Magnum is a tall rum and coke with lime for just $7.25—and regulars know to order Double Magnums. There's also a listing of TCP Bombs, various shots served with a Monster energy drink back. And yes, Chartreuse is one of the options.

A film still of Kurt Russell hangs on the wall right above a Chartreuse poster in the corner where that Death Proof scene was filmed, and Tarantino still comes by for a visit whenever he's in town. Clint Eastwood, Robert Plant, and countless others have also spent time at the Chili Parlor. "If someone comes into town, you bring 'em here," declares Zoob matter-of-factly. "Where else you gonna bring 'em, some new shit bar?"

THE CLOAK ROOM

1300 Colorado Street
Austin, TX 78701

As I'm walking toward the Cloak Room one January afternoon, I see masses of suits and ties migrating from the Capitol. It's not until I descend the stairs into the little underground haunt and my eyes adjust to the darkness that it hits me: it's the first day of the 88th Texas Legislative session. This historic establishment, which celebrated its 50th birthday in 2022, normally gets a good amount of traffic from the Capitol, but it's buzzing non-stop at this time of year with politicians who are both seeking refuge and talking shop. It's safe to say that many political deals have been made over a tipple or two in this dark space.

"Everything at the Cloak Room stays at the Cloak Room," says Melissa Pruitt, who's been running the bar for the last six years, taking over for her mother Beverly, who ran it from 1989 before retiring in 2021. "She ran a tight ship, she was real stern," says Pruitt of her mother, who was invited to attend Obama's second inauguration. "You ever watch Cheers? There's a Carla in every bar."

The Cloak Room is located in the bottom level of the Victorian Goodman Building, the first floor of which had originally been built to house stonecutters working on the statehouse when it was being built in the 1880s. But

it was in the late 1970s that Ed Baxter, a lobbyist for Blue Cross/Blue Shield with an office upstairs, decided that the Capitol needed a bar like the ones he'd experienced on Capitol Hill. Baxter put out an ad in the newspaper seeking an operator for a new bar and 24-year-old Jim LeMond, a UT student, answered. LeMond turned the dirt cellar into the bar it is today and went on to become a legend in the Austin bar world before opening Barton Springs Saloon (page 276) several decades later. The Cloak Room has changed hands many times through the years, and when one of the last owners passed away and willed it to a family member who didn't want it, nine members of Phi Gamma Delta took over the lease. Bev was already running the bar, and that's exactly how they wanted to keep it.

DRINK LIKE A LOCAL: AUSTIN

Not much has changed here through the years. An intricate architectural drawing of the Capitol acts as a centerpiece against the wood and mirror-paneled walls, which are lit by shaded bronze wall sconces. A jukebox at the entrance provides the nightly soundtrack, with options like B.B. King, Hank Williams, Lionel Richie, and Bob Seger. Swinging saloon doors lead to the bathroom stairs, and the walls on the way up are plastered with years' worth of patron photos. There's a modest selection of bottles behind the bar, with Tito's and soda, and Macallan or Woodford Reserve on the rocks being the top orders. Pruitt always provides some kind of food for happy hour, whether it's cheese and crackers, mixed nuts, or her homemade meatballs, made famous by local radio station KLBJ.

"I like to make them feel like they're at home, that's the main thing," says Pruitt, taking a drag of her cigarette at her usual spot just outside the entrance. "I think that's why they like the vibe so much."

SMALL VICTORY

108 E 7th Street
Austin, TX 78701

Converting one of Austin's oldest buildings into a bar for the first time is no small feat, as industry veteran Josh Loving quickly learned after obtaining a 19th-century livery stable-turned-parking-garage attached to the Stephen F. Austin Royal Sonesta Hotel.

"When we really got into the demolition and construction process, at times it felt like it was one step forward, two or three steps back," remembers Loving. "It was like peeling a rotten onion. My partner Brian Stubbs said, 'If we get this bar open in this space, it'll be a small victory.'" And so it was.

This was the first bar project for Loving, who served as the wine buyer for beloved, now-shuttered Mediterranean restaurant Fino before working on the opening team for some of the city's top cocktail bars—like Midnight Cowboy and the sorely missed Austin location of New York-based Weather Up. When planning out Small Victory, he drew inspiration from neo-speakeasies like Milk & Honey, Dutch Kills, Little Branch, and Franklin Mortgage & Investment Co.

"The quality of the finished product is the top priority," says Loving. "We keep our glasses frozen, our tools are kept cold, all of our water is softened and filtered, and we're very deliberate about the products we offer. We

choose our spirits based on whether they are quality enough to sip on their own at room temperature."

Small Victory is one of the only bars in town to pioneer their own ice program, using an electric chainsaw to break down 300-pound blocks into more manageable "loaves," which are then cut on a butcher's bandsaw into rocks, spears, punch blocks, and shaking rocks.

Since opening at the start of 2016, Loving had been building up a diverse collection of rum and brandy, though he says they've been consistently challenging to source post-COVID due to glass shortages and shipping issues. The cocktail menu is focused on classics, from the more familiar Singapore Sling to the lesser-known Don Lockwood No. 2, made with tequila reposado, mezcal, maple, Angostura, and chocolate bitters. They also offer a large-format punch bowl, a listing of low-ABV options, and hand-cut cheese and charcuterie.

The vintage design of the intimate space is at once classy and cozy, with navy subway tile behind the bar, light blue banquettes and matching swivel bar seat, fire hydrant and parking meter toile wallpaper, a large round booth in the back under a portrait of JFK, and colorful Tiffany-style lamps aglow against wood-paneled walls. It's the kind of place to bring a first date; it's almost guaranteed to lead to another.

SINGAPORE SLING

This classic cocktail has a debatable origin but is said to have been created in 1915 by Ngiam Tong Boon at the Long Bar in Singapore's Raffles Hotel. Small Victory's version is elevated with the best versions of spirits and a grenadine made in-house with pomegranate juice, sugar, hibiscus, and orange flower water. It has been on the menu since the bar's first day, and they've sold more of these than any other drink.

1½ oz. London dry gin (Tanqueray 10 if you want to be fancy)

¼ oz. grenadine

¼ oz. Benedictine

¼ oz. Cointreau

½ oz. Heering cherry liqueur

½ oz. fresh lime juice

1½ oz. fresh pineapple juice

1 dash bitters

Soda water, to top

Pineapple wedge, to garnish

Maraschino cherry, to garnish

1. Build all the ingredients into the short tin of a shaker set.

2. Add ice to a large shaker tin, pour ingredients over the ice, seal the tins, and shake briefly.

3. Prepare a Collins glass with ice; a single 5 x 1¼ x 1¼ spear is what they use at Small Victory.

4. Top up with soda and garnish with the pineapple wedge and maraschino cherry.

FIREHOUSE LOUNGE

605 Brazos Street
Austin, TX 78701

Downtown Austin bartenders put out a lot of proverbial fires. But back in Austin's early days, the site now housing Firehouse Lounge was putting out literal ones. The aptly named bar was originally home to the two-story Washington #1 Station, built in 1885 in tandem with the Driskill Hotel. Back then, it was run by a group of volunteer firefighters who used horse-drawn carriages, and then steam-powered engines. Sometime in the 1920s, a third story was added and the exterior was updated to more of an Art Deco style.

When Collin Ballard and his business partner Kent Roth took over the space in 2012, the upstairs was a vacant office space and the downstairs was an underground dubstep bar called Rocco's. They did a hasty two-week rehab of the space to open in time for South by Southwest—the city's biggest music and film festival—that March, launching with a 5-day music showcase featuring over 30 bands and an art gallery upstairs. By SXSW 2013, the second level had become Firehouse Hostel, and guests were now able to enter the bar through a hidden door disguised as a bookshelf in the hostel's lobby.

The mood changes as soon as you slip into the space, which is sultry with red velveteen damask wallpaper, black tufted booths, and the soft glow from Edison lightbulb sconces and classic glass votives typically found in red sauce Italian joints. Guests are asked to mind a list of rules, which range from "buy a round for your friends: it feels good" to "do not bring anyone unless you would leave that person alone in your home." A few stairs lead down into the center of the room, where high-top tables face a small stage. Depending on the night, you might stumble upon a salsa band, hip hop DJ, or blues trio.

"I like to think Firehouse is the perfect place to pull up a stool and tell the bartender what you're in the mood for," says Ballard. "They've always been amazing at crafting something on a whim and with less bravado than some of the stuffier cocktail lounges around. We're a little divey, and we love it."

Well-made, no-nonsense drinks at reasonable prices—it's no wonder Firehouse Lounge has become an industry hangout too.

HERE NOR THERE & IN PLAIN SIGHT

612 Brazos Street
Austin, TX 78701

When Here Nor There (HNT) opened in June 2018, the subterranean cocktail bar was immediately shrouded in mystery. The speakeasy, with a hidden location and a coded door, was originally described as a members only club—and by invitation only. Out of the gate, they were crafting some of the best drinks in the city, yet no big bar-world names seemed to be associated with the project. That is because HNT is, incredibly, born-and-raised Austinite Manish Patel's very first venture in hospitality.

While traveling frequently for business in his 20s and 30s, Patel had been a regular at cocktail bars and boutique hotels around the world. After seeing major success with his sports nutrition company Cellucor, as well as a freight brokerage company for which he is a capital co-founder, he decided to invest in hospitality. He connected with bar consultant Terance Robson at a London bar called Trailer Happiness and together they assembled a team of bartenders who'd worked at some of the best cocktail bars in the world, bringing them to Austin on temporary visas. Now, with bar and hotel projects on the horizon in Austin, Houston, and New York, he's working on getting them permanent citizenship.

"I wanted to find the friendliest people who are skilled at what they do and then wow the customer by giving them a consistent experience that is beyond anything else they've ever experienced," says Patel. "We wanted to be a word-of-mouth brand. I believe that, if you treat people right and give them an amazing experience, they'll tell ten other people."

Patel already owned the building on the corner of 7th and Brazos, a historically important site where The

American and The Statesman merged to become The Austin-American Statesman in 1924. He dug the bar out of the blue limestone under the building, then coffee-stained the original brick found in the process and used it for the bar's interior walls. Silver plates from all over the world overlap across one entire wall, in an homage to the bar's global influences, and a tree installation, made from vines scavenged off Texas ranches, fill the corners. Velvet pillows and mood lighting set the sultry scene for enjoying the bar's truly memorable drinks with someone special.

In addition to a menu of favorite drinks that have become classics, HNT features a rotating conceptual menu. Beverage director Conor O'Reilly takes the lead on these creations, and the whole team collaborates to fine-tune each cocktail. Their approach is remarkably culinary, using methods more commonly found in kitchens than bars; for example, sous vide is used frequently as a more controlled way of infusing flavors. The signature Milk & Honey cocktail, which takes a full 24 hours to create, is a rum punch that uses clarified whole milk to add flavor and texture. Ice is shaved to order off a large block at the bar, and glassware is meticulously selected to match each liquid creation. Spirits purists will marvel at the curated collection behind the bar, including Glenfiddich 50, one of the rarest bottles of Scotch in the world.

In July 2022, the team opened In Plain Sight on the street level of the same building, in an intimate 16-person capacity space: 8 seats and 8 standing spots. Recessed angled ceiling panels with color changing LED lights allow the bartenders to set the mood, often informed by the music coming through the sound system. The focus here is on aperitif and digestif cocktails, like the Open Sesame—Japanese whisky, clarified coconut, toasted sesame seeds, and soda—and the Poppy Lou Paloma—mezcal, coconut-infused rum, spice mix, clarified grapefruit juice, and elderflower. Both cocktails are crystal clear, minimalist in presentation, and layered with perfectly balanced and complementary flavors.

Here Nor There is no longer members-only, though existing members do get preference for reservations on busy nights. Make a reservation request using their app and, once accepted, you'll be provided with the gate code for access. But if they're booked up, I suggest sidling up to the marble bar at In Plain Sight. Make friends with the bartenders and they might be able to work some magic for you downstairs. Or you may have such a great time upstairs, you'll want to stay put.

SLÁINTE

This Irish coffee rendition was inspired by the HNT team's love of a British dessert called the Banoffee pie, made from bananas, cream toffee, and coffee on a buttery biscuit base. One of their Irish bartenders had missed home while learning his craft in London and regularly made himself an Irish coffee to finish the days. On a cold winter evening, he enjoyed one alongside his first-ever Banoffee pie and immediately conceptualized this spin on an already-perfect drink: banana cream, Guinness and vanilla syrup, dark robust coffee, and smooth Irish whiskey.

½ oz. Guinness

1 splash of vanilla extract

1 oz. Jameson Irish Whiskey

2 oz. Figure 8 Coffee

3 oz. heavy whipping cream

1 oz. Banane du Bresil

1. Combine the Guinness and vanilla in a saucepan and reduce over medium heat for about 15 minutes, or until thickened.
2. Add the whiskey and coffee to the saucepan, stir, and pour into a 6 oz. Irish coffee glass.
3. In a bowl, combine the cream and Banane Du Bresil and blend well to create a banana cream floater to top the drink.

More Locally Loved Capitol Area and Central Congress Avenue Bars:

HIGHER GROUND
720 Congress Avenue, Austin, TX 78701

THE ELEPHANT ROOM
315 Congress Avenue, Austin, TX 78701

SWIFT'S ATTIC
315 Congress Avenue, Suite 200, Austin, TX 78701

MORT SUBITE
308 Congress Avenue, Austin, TX 78701

ELLIS
111 Congress Avenue, Austin, TX 78701

P6 AT THE LINE AUSTIN
111 E César Chávez Street, Austin, TX 78701

WAREHOUSE DISTRICT

The Warehouse District refers to the grid of streets stretching roughly from Congress Avenue to Nueces Street, between West César Chávez and West 6th Street. In the 19th century, this industrial area of town was built along the freight rail lines running between 3rd and 4th Streets, and was once filled with lumberyards, dry goods stores, breweries, and factories. Nicknamed "Guy Town," it was also known for its bordellos, or "female boarding houses." The Vulcan Gas Company, Austin's legendary psychedelic music venue, opened at the edge of the district on 3rd and Congress in the late 1960s, now a Patagonia. The area west of Congress remained industrial well into the 1970s, when the fabled rock venue Liberty Lunch opened on West 2nd Street. It was the pioneering gay bars that transformed the Warehouse District into a bustling entertainment district in the 1980s.

Unfortunately, very few historical protections were ever put in place to ensure that the neighborhood is preserved. Large turn-of-the-century warehouses housing bars like The Bitter End, Ginger Man, and Fox and Hound have already been razed and redeveloped with residential high-rises and hotels. In 2000, the city developed West 2nd Street into a high-end shopping district, and the current Austin City Hall opened its doors in 2004, followed by Austin City Limits Live at the Moody Theater. While some local businesses, like Lamberts, La Condesa, Toy Joy, and Violet Crown Cinema, have survived, locations of corporate chains are beginning to open in the 2nd Street District as smaller operations close due to rising rent. Now, the city's only LGBTQ+ district is facing extinction as an approved development is planning a 40-story residential building at West 4th and Colorado. At press time, Oilcan Harry's is in talks with the developer, who supposedly intends to work the city's oldest gay bar into the new development, but surrounding gay bars like Rain, Coconut Club, and Neon Grotto face an uncertain future.

THE ROOSEVELT ROOM

307 W 5th Street
Austin, TX 78701

After coming up in the service industry in Boulder, Colorado, Justin Lavenue moved down to Austin and started working at premiere bars like Half Step (page 238) and DrinkWell, with the intention of opening his own bar one day. And when he met Dennis Gobis, a German-born hospitality veteran, the two started to put that plan in motion. They found a perfect space at the northern edge of the Warehouse District, originally built as a railway warehouse in 1929.

They did a quick turnaround on the two-level club that had been there previously. They kept the bar tops—marble upstairs and soapstone downstairs, lit from below to illuminate the drinks—but replaced the crushed red velvet booth upholstery with black leather, installed a wall of bricks blackened in the Chicago Fires, and hung black and white paintings of musicians Miles Davis and Gary Clark Jr., the late bar guru Sasha Petraske, and Eleanor Roosevelt.

"She was the ultimate egalitarian," says Lavenue. "She treated everyone with respect and love and that's a big part of what Dennis and I wanted to do when we opened this bar."

They decided to call the concept The Roosevelt Room, named after the president when Prohibition was repealed, and named the adjacent event space The Eleanor. They planned on renting out the space for some events and cocktail pop-ups to generate income before closing to lay out a detailed business plan and intentionally relaunch. But things didn't go quite as planned. When Lavenue won a Bombay Sapphire cocktail competition in September 2015, the bar blew up overnight. They began accepting reservations and moved to a table service model, and the awards kept rolling in.

They're still serving some of the city's best cocktails, and producing top bartenders thanks to a rigorous training program, starting with a required minimum of three months to a year of serving or bar-backing before even getting behind the bar, regardless of prior experience. Next, they train twice weekly for six months to a year, with the goal of building a round of ten cocktails at a time— and spending less than a minute per drink. That's impressive enough, but more so when you watch them in elegant action behind the bar.

"We have a staff that works very hard and takes this very seriously," says Lavenue. "They want to do this as their profession. 38 of our 40 employees are full-time."

A visit to The Roosevelt Room is like a lesson in cocktail history. There's over 80 of them on the menu: House Creations conceptualized by members of the staff; Classic Creations, House Creations that have become so popular they never left the menu; Featured Indulgences, seasonal offerings that change through the year; and By The Era, 53 classic cocktails divided into seven major drinking eras, from the Early Years (pre-1880) to Modern Classics (2000 to present). Even these classics have been given their own Roosevelt twist and meticulously refined to perfection. For example, the Mai Tai is made with a touch of amontillado sherry for nuttiness, and the Saturn is made more complex with both pisco and yuzu. There's also a "President's" version of each cocktail, made with even higher quality spirits. For example, the President's Bobby Burns, made with 30-year Speyside Scotch, will run you $750.

Try all 53 of the By The Era cocktails and you become a Board Member, earning a shiny gold plaque on the board above the bar. But try all 53 President's versions and you join the exclusive President's Club, which gets you your own presidential portrait painted and hung in the bar. One regular has already made his way through the entire Presidential collection and is on round two; Lavenue is currently seeking an artist to sculpt him a well-earned bust.

"Roosevelt literally has been a work in progress since day one," says Lavenue. "Every time you walk in, there will be something new about this place...We're planning a big revamp of the space in the next year or two, to breathe new life into it for the next seven to ten years."

THE PHARAOH'S DANCE

The Pharaoh's Dance currently resides on the Classic Creations menu, and was created by Alex Shoemaker for the Miles Davis Kind of Blue album tribute, performed by The Ephraim Owens Quintet at Roosevelt Room in July 2015. With a beautiful balance of green herbs, acidity, and gentle sweetness, it has remained a well-loved house cocktail.

¾ oz. Beefeater 24 Dry Gin

½ oz. Thai Basil Syrup

½ oz. lychee juice

¼ oz. St-Germain

¼ teaspoon St. George Absinthe

½ oz. fresh lemon juice

1-2 oz. Stone IPA

Lemon wheel, to garnish

Thai basil sprig, to garnish

Grated nutmeg, to garnish

1. Combine all of the ingredients, except the beer, in a cocktail shaker with ice, short shake, and single strain into a hurricane glass over crushed ice.

2. Insert a metal straw, top with the beer and crushed ice.

3. Garnish with a lemon wheel against the back of the glass, a basil sprig in front of the lemon wheel, and top with grated nutmeg.

Thai Basil Syrup: In a blender, combine 20g Thai basil leaves, 500ml sugar, and 500ml water and blend on high for 5 minutes, until the sugar is fully dissolved. Strain through a cheesecloth, pressing gently to extract as much liquid as possible from the solids. Pour into a bottle and cover tightly with a cap. Refrigerate to store.

GARAGE

503 Colorado Street
Austin, TX 78701

Austin has its fair share of hidden bars, but Garage takes the cake as far as unexpected locations go. It's set inside a parking garage on Colorado between 5th Street and 6th Street, in the building where the American National Bank opened in 1954 as the city's first example of mid-century modern urban architecture. Once you arrive, you'll see "enter" and "exit" signs for the garage, but you'll want to follow the sign that reads "cocktails" and the bar's glowing blue neon sign.

The entranceway—now furnished with brown leather seating and candlelit marble bar tops against the building's original brick and blue tile—is where the valets used to wait for bank customers to bring their cars. They'd drive them to the rooftop garage, then slide down six floors on a fireman's pole—look up at the entrance and you can see the circular space where the pole used to be—and hand the keys back to the attendant through a small window.

Real estate developer William Ball saw the potential for this space and collaborated with a number of partners, including renowned chef Phillip Speer, to open Garage Bar in 2014. Interior designer Micki Spencer, known for her work at other bars and restaurants like Ah Sing Den, Hillside Farmacy, and Eberly, created an understated-but-elegant environment complementing the building's original concrete and brick with a palette of browns and greys, marble tables, leather and tweed

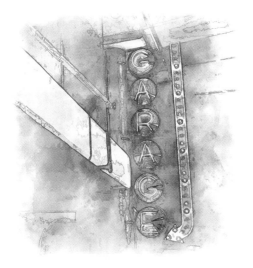

mid-century furniture, and Edison fixtures.

"In many ways, there's a sense of timelessness when you come here," says general manager Chris Simpson. "You're stepping out from the hustle and bustle of downtown Austin, into this hidden space. You kind of lose track of where you are and you're just here in it."

Nothing but vinyl plays through the hi-fi system, rotating through several hundred records plus selections their audiophile employees bring in. Simpson says the rounded bar, and intentional roundedness of the space in general, makes for great acoustics. The intimate space is perfect for date nights, and they are always sure not to pack it too full and risk sacrificing the guest experience.

The spirits program is whiskey-focused, with a huge selection of bourbon, rye, scotch, and Japanese whisky, including desirable bottles like Hibiki 21, Eagle Rare, and Pappy 23. The cocktails change seasonally and include plenty of non-alcoholic options so that everyone is included. If it's your first visit, definitely try the signature Indian Paintbrush, once named the Official Drink of Austin by the Texas Food & Wine Alliance: a simple yet timeless blend of vodka, rosemary, grapefruit, and lime. If you're feeling peckish, they also offer snacks like salsa macha popcorn and spiced pecans.

"The cocktails, the ambiance, the experience, the hospitality: all of those for us have to be at the same level without compromising one for another," says Simpson. "The space is great but it's our character that keeps people coming back."

AUTUMN SWEATER

This cocktail was created in reverence to the Yo La Tengo song "Autumn Sweater." The song plays on the themes of insecurity and nakedness felt early on in an intimate relationship; the "autumn sweater" represents comfort and security in those early stages of vulnerability. The cocktail itself is simple in its presentation and comforting in its familiarity. As such, it is a great gateway for those who are newly entering the world of cocktails, or those overwhelmed by overly boozy or complex drinks.

1½ oz. white rum

½ oz. pear eau de vie

¾ oz. fresh lime juice

½ oz. Cinnamon-Turbinado Syrup

Grated cinnamon, to garnish

1. Combine all of the ingredients in a cocktail shaker with ice, shake well, and double strain into a coupe.

2. Garnish with the grated cinnamon.

Cinnamon-Turbinado Syrup: In a saucepan, add 1 oz. cinnamon sticks to 10 oz. water and bring to a boil. Add 10 oz. turbinado sugar, lower heat, and simmer for 5 minutes. Remove from heat, let cool, and then pour into a container and refrigerate overnight. The next day, strain and store.

PÉCHÉ

208 W 4th Street
Austin, TX 78701

When Péché opened in the Warehouse District in 2008, the craft cocktail movement was a twinkle in the city's proverbial eye. Rob Pate, who got his start in the service industry 40 years ago, managed the now-closed brewpub The Bitter End before operating Cedar Street Courtyard for 15 years, when the space now housing Péché became available. He'd always wanted to open a bistro—"good, simple food done incredibly well," he says, his favorite. But when absinthe became legal in the States six months before he launched his new concept, he decided to open as an absinthe-focused bar specializing in pre-Prohibition cocktails—and named it Péché, which means "sin" in French.

Step inside this incredible 115-year-old former ware-house space, and it feels like you could very well be in a Parisian bistro. Péché's walls, made of exposed sandstone brick, are ornamented with wall sconces, scalloped mirrors, and absinthe ads. Guests can choose from small bistro tables spaced out across the well-loved wooden floorboards or slip into tufted mint-green booths. Custom gaslight-inspired lamps from New Orleans light the bar top, which is lined with vintage absinthe fountains. A rolling ladder runs the span of the back bar, which has become a bona fide spirits library over the years, containing over a dozen different types of absinthe, plus gems like 75-year-old Pierre Ferrand cognac and 50-year-old Glenfiddich.

In a city where several French concepts have opened and closed through the years, Péché is still holding strong with its menu of classic staples like escargot, Croque Madame, steak tartare, and seared foie gras, plus seasonal specials. "I'm an old barman who got lucky and figured out the food pretty quick," says Pate matter-of-factly.

Péché's cocktail menu, which is split up by primary spirits, leans heavy on the classics but also includes Péché's own variations, like the iconic Fig Manhattan (a Manhattan topped with fig foam) and Rosemary's Gimlet, a gimlet crowned with flamed rosemary. During happy hour, which runs all day on Mondays and Tuesdays and 4-7 p.m. Wednesday through Saturday, select cocktails dip down to an unbelievable $6—surely one of the best deals in town.

"When we first opened up, I led everything [behind the bar], but now the kids do it," says Pate, referring to his staff. He's helped some of the top bartenders in town get their start before they moved on to open concepts of their own. "I used to teach everybody when they came in, and now these guys teach me a few things. But every now and then they find out the old man really knows what's back there."

RED HEADED STEPCHILD

119 E 5th Street
Austin, TX 78701

POV: You approach the Fifth Street sign advertising Floppy Disk Repair Co., and punch four numbers into the keypad by the door, fingers crossed that the code you were given at the last bar is correct. Success! You've made it into the appropriately dark and red-lit space known as Red Headed Stepchild.

Bloody dolls and one-eyed plush animals peer down at you from every corner of the bar and you'll spot taxidermy in unexpected places—some muzzled, or two-headed, or draped with pentagrams and disco balls. Hexagon flooring mimics the carpeting from The Shining, a stabby ax serves as the handle to the bathroom door, and the creepy words "your hair smells pretty" are spelled out in neon.

Brett Vance and Willie Stark, starting as a dishwasher and a waiter, respectively, worked their way up through the bar industry, accruing 20 years of hospitality industry experience, before opening HandleBar in 2012, followed by Red Headed Stepchild in 2016. And they didn't exactly plan for it to be a serial killer-themed bar. It just sort of... happened.

"Willie has red hair, so it was a term he heard a lot growing up and felt like he could have some fun with

it," explained Vance. "So we designed the Red Headed Stepchild around a mischievous little kid. Think the movie Problem Child, but for some reason as the decor was picked out, it just kept getting creepier and more murderous, and eventually we decided he was a little serial killer child. So, we designed somewhere that we thought the serial killer child would like to hang out...and oddly enough neither of us really likes horror movies."

You're in luck if you can snag one of the swing seats at the bar. This is the prime location for enjoying their cheekily named cocktails and tasting notes: like the Lean in my Cup— "tastes like fly women and fancy things," made with dark rum, cinnamon syrup, grape Fanta, and lime; or It's Your Fault I'm a Stripper, Daddy—"tastes like rolled up one-dollar bills," made with mezcal, rhubarb amaro, sarsaparilla bitters, and coconut milk.

Just this year, they opened a new concept on the eastside called Mama Dearest. The small space is filled with taxidermy, retro beer ads, rawhide lampshades, creepy doll heads, vintage Playboy magazines, clotheslines filled with laundry, and all sorts of ghostly ephemera and intriguing curios, lit by the sparkle of a spinning disco ball.

"The thought behind Mama Dearest was actually, where did the red headed stepchild grow up?" explains Vance. "We settled on a backwoods cabin and described it as Mommie Dearest meets Deliverance to our designers. So both bars are kinda cozy and fucked up at the same time."

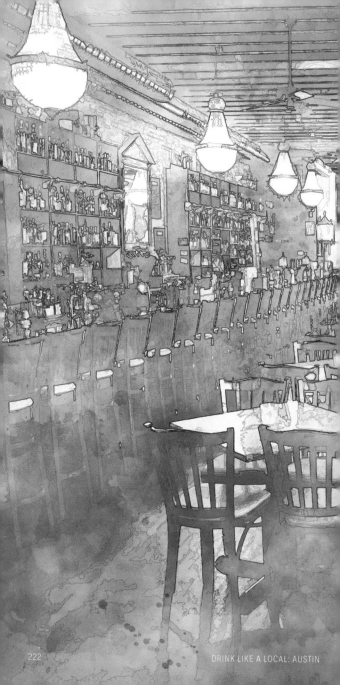

More Locally Loved Warehouse District Bars:

KALIMOTXO
607 W 3rd Street, #105, Austin, TX 78701

LAVACA STREET BAR
405 Lavaca Street, Austin, TX 78701

HALCYON
218 W 4th Street, Austin, TX 78701

RAIN
217 W 4th Street, Austin, TX 78701

DUMONT'S DOWN LOW
214 W 4th Street, Suite B, Austin, TX 78701

OILCAN HARRY'S
211 W 4th Street, Austin, TX 78701

NEON GROTTO
318 Colorado Street, Austin, TX 78701

COCONUT CLUB
310B Colorado Street, Austin, TX 78701

CEDAR DOOR
201 Brazos Street, Building A, Austin, TX 78701

RED RIVER STREET

Red River Street is another part of downtown that has lived many lives. In the city's earliest days, it was home to wagon yards, followed by automobile businesses. In the early 20th century, it became known as an antiques row, with antiques dealers setting up shop alongside dressmakers and shoemakers. By the 1950s, the street was dominated by junk shops and used furniture stores, and it started to fall into disrepair along with 6th Street. One of the first clubs to open up on Red River was the New Orleans Club, where the 13th Floor Elevators made their debut in 1966. Next door, at a venue called 11th Door, Janis Joplin and Jerry Jeff Walker performed. More bars and clubs continued to pop up on the street, which had incidentally earned quite a reputation for drugs and prostitution. By the 1980s, the edgy district was lined with grungy places hosting mostly punk acts at venues like Cave Club and the lawless BYOB Cavity Club. In the mid-1990s, Stubb's Bar-B-Q moved from Lubbock to Austin and opened its now-famous restaurant on Red

Dripping
Spri

Driftwood

Hays

River before expanding the backyard into Waller Creek Amphitheater, truly solidifying the street as a live music district. While the names and ownership of many of the venues have changed through the years, several have gone on to become institutions, such as Elysium and Mohawk. In 2013, the section of Red River from 6th Street to 10th Street was designated a cultural district by the Texas Commission for the Arts. On any given night, you can catch live music at any of the many venues lining the street.

Once Red River crosses 6th Street, it changes quite drastically as it nears the Austin Convention Center before leading into the Rainey Street district. While the west side of the Convention Center is hugged by chain restaurants, like most convention center districts, the Red River side is home to the historic Iron Works Barbecue, which opened in 1978, the speakeasy Kinfolk (page 230) set in one of the oldest buildings in Austin, and Central District Brewing, the very first brewery to open downtown since the closing of The Bitter End and Lovejoy's.

CHEER UP CHARLIES

900 Red River Street
Austin, TX 78701

It's like an Austin rite of passage: Do you remember when Waterloo Video stood where Lululemon now resides? Or before REI replaced the flagship Whole Foods Market downtown? Or when Lovejoy's served its very last pint of homebrew? Then you also must remember when Cheer Up Charlies opened as a little trailer slinging kombucha, young coconuts, and raw chocolate on East 6th Street. In 2010, they upgraded to a brick-and-mortar with a liquor license, taking over a little shanty of a biker-bar-turned-DIY-punk-venue known as Ms. Bea's.

When news broke in late 2013 that the 600 square foot space was closing because its landlords had sold the property to be developed into a hotel, it was met with outrage from the community. At the time, Cheer Up Charlies was the only bar of its kind on the eastside: a space where truly everyone was not only welcome but celebrated. To call it a "gay bar" seems restrictive—it's always been much more than that; think of it as the embodiment of "y'all means all" long before that phrase started appearing on T-shirts and pins around town.

Owners Tamara Hoover and Maggie Lea put out a fare-well message, assuring that they'd find another space and reopen. Sure enough, a couple months later, the bar relaunched on 9th and Red River, in the space formerly occupied by Club Deville—and, before that, a lesbian bar called Chances. Not only was Cheer Ups, as regulars call it, reviving a piece of LGBTQ+ history, but it was able to grow into a full-fledged venue with a sprawling patio and indoor and outdoor bars and stages.

Over a decade later, Cheer Up Charlies is still thriving in this space, where it's splashed with layers of colorful murals and hosts countless live music performances, drag shows, and voguing competitions on its main outdoor stage, which is flanked by an iconic rainbow-lit rock wall. With vegan truck Arlo's parked outside and signature drinks flowing inside, like their Kale Margarita and the Golden Ticket—always my go-to, made with whiskey, kombucha, lavender bitters, and candied gin-ger. You might even feel healthier going home than you did at the start of your night—no promises though.

THE SIDE BAR

602 E 7th Street
Austin, TX 78701

I'll never forget my first South by Southwest, in 2006. I'd moved to Austin several months before the March music festival and had no idea what to expect. When I started walking around from bar to bar, I quickly realized I'd made a rookie mistake by failing to RSVP to all the free parties that were taking place throughout downtown. And that's how I ended up at The Side Bar for the first time. The 7th Street bar welcomed me with open arms and strong drinks—and hasn't stopped since.

I got such a feeling of familiarity from the place when I first walked in, it seemed like it had been there for years already. But Austinites Trey Spaw and Soo Lee-Spaw had only opened the bar in 2004.

"We had both been raised and worked in the service industry most of our lives and it was finally at the point where we wanted to be our own bosses," Lee-Spaw remembers. So they began scouting affordable downtown locations—three words you no longer see together in Austin. "We were tipped off by the Elysium owner, John Wickham, that our current location sat empty and had not been occupied since the 1980s—except for mounds of asbestos and some risque posters from a long-ago club called B's Leather Chaine Drive, and a giant hole in the roof!"

They took the leap and spent all their savings, along with a personal family loan, to invest in a remodel and

opened the bar in ten months thanks to many handy friends who helped them paint, build things, and set up the bar. The font for the iconic sign outside was purchased from a type designer, to honor his work, and Lee-Spaw said she'll never forget how many blisters she got from hand cutting those letters with tin scissors.

Side Bar got its name because it was just on the other side of Red River clubs, a perfect place for drinks before or after shows. While spots like Beerland, Red Eyed Fly, and Room 710 are long shuttered, venues like Mohawk, Cheer Up Charlie's, 13th Floor, CHESS CLUB, and Elysium are thriving.

You'll still make random friends out on the buzzing patio and the bathrooms are tagged up as ever, but now plants, vintage furniture, and framed screen-printed posters give the bar a classy, homey feel. And though Banzai, the beloved Italian blues harmonica player who manned the door for a decade, moved on during the pandemic, Side Bar still has the cheap pool tables, legendary jukebox, and stiff drinks for which they are known.

"We keep it simple and are known for our generous pours," says Lee-Spaw. "A regular even entered a definition in Urban Dictionary. Look up 'sidebar pour.'"

KINFOLK

303 B Red River Street
Austin, TX

Nestled between the Red River entertainment district and the drinking street that is Rainey, you'll find Kinfolk. Or, more specifically, you'll check in at the host stand at Moonshine Grill—the city's iconic Southern comfort restaurant—and be escorted down a stairway leading to a cellar. On your way down, take in the sights: stained glass depicting a still, old bourbon barrel heads, and framed Prohibition-era art. When you arrive at the door, you might want to peek through the eye-level window to fully get in character before entering the space. Now you've arrived at Kinfolk.

Moonshine Grill is housed in a part of the old Waterloo Compound, an original grouping of some of the very oldest commercial buildings in Austin built in 1852 by a German settler named Henry F. Hofheintz. During the pandemic, the cellar floor needed repairing. Moonshine owners, and longtime restaurateurs, Larry Perdido and Chuck Smith opened a Pandora's box when they removed the flooring in what was originally a storm cellar, and then a wine cellar under the restaurant, built by legendary chef Charlie Trotter when it was his restaurant called Emilia's.

"The next evolution of the space wasn't about rebuilding a wine room but creating a space and concept that aligned with the southern concept operating above," explains Perdido. "Enter Kinfolk, a space that embraced the idea of serving up proper cocktails and proper pours

from an extensive spirit library."

Hand-cut limestone walls from the mid-1800s serve as a backdrop to the most highly curated spirit list in the city. Kinfolk is home to over 700 different spirits, collected by the owners over two decades, and most of them can be viewed around a long communal table in the "spirits library." You'll find everything from single malt Japanese whisky to Austrian schnapps to Italian amaro to Brazilian cachaça, all available to sip 1.5 ounces at a time. The cocktail menu is a "family tree" of sorts, featuring five categories—Fancy Drinks, Sours, Bucks, Old Fashioned & Improved, and Daisies—and the genesis of each cocktail from its ancestral version into the classic and modern iterations.

The intimate 20-seat space, which opened at the very end of 2021, may sound exclusive—and it is—but it also feels incredibly welcoming. Round marble tables and leather barrel chairs are perfect for date nights, the staff will passionately wax poetic about each cocktail presented in perfectly elegant glassware, and wall sconces and votive candles give the space a warm glow.

MANHATTAN

The foundation of Kinfolk's cocktail program is formed by many canonical creations of the eighteenth and nineteenth centuries. Nearly every one of these seminal drinks is characterized by origins that are difficult to pin down with objective certainty, so the bar team at Kinfolk lets ambiguity open the door to interpretation.

Angostura's aromatic bitters are included in some of the first printed Manhattan recipes from 1884; the precedent for using rye whiskey was purportedly first established in the 1887 posthumously published third edition of Jerry Thomas's Bartenders Guide; and the presumed first appearance of a cherry garnish appeared in 1891 in the Kansas City Times. For the inclusion of orange liqueur, they looked not only to Manhattan recipes from 1884 to 1891, but also to the groundbreaking New York City speakeasy Employees Only, which opened in 2004. Their house Manhattan is still prepared with Grand Marnier "Cordon Rouge," so Kinfolk's version of the recipe nods to the East Coast by including Grand Marnier's "Cuvée Louis Alexandre": a version of the original liqueur that is less sweet and features older Cognac brandies in the blend.

Todd Smith's 2005 Black Manhattan derivation came from San Francisco's Bourbon & Branch, and that is what inspired Kinfolk to replace sweet red vermouth with an Italian bitter liqueur. Instead of Smith's prescribed Averna amaro, they opted for the presence of mandarin oranges, gentian, sage, cinnamon, ginger, and chamomile found in Foro amaro from the La Canellese distillery in Calamandrana, Piemonte. With influences from coast to coast, Kinfolk's Manhattan serves as a tribute to both the past and present of American bartending.

2 oz. Russell's Reserve 6 Year Old Kentucky straight rye whiskey

¼ oz. Grand Marnier "Cuvée Louis Alexandre" liqueur

¾ oz. Foro Amaro Speciale Liqueur

3 dashes bitters

1 Fabbri Amarena cherry, to garnish

1. Add ice to the mixing glass, followed by ingredients.

2. Stir, then strain into a chilled coupe.

3. Place the cherry into the glass as a garnish.

More Locally Loved Red River Bars, Breweries, and Venues:

MOHAWK
912 Red River Street, Austin, TX 78701

STUBB'S BAR-B-Q
801 Red River Street, Austin, TX 78701

BETTER DAYS
714 Red River Street, Austin, TX 78701

VALHALLA
710 Red River Street, Austin, TX 78701

THE 13TH FLOOR
711 Red River Street, Austin, TX 78701

ELYSIUM
705 Red River Street, Austin, TX 78701

CHESS CLUB
617 Red River Street, Austin, TX 78701

SWAN DIVE
615 Red River Street, Austin, TX 78701

CENTRAL DISTRICT BREWING
417 Red River Street, Austin, TX 78701

RAINEY STREET

When cattle baron Jesse Driskill, founder of The Driskill Hotel, and physician Frank Rainey first developed Rainey Street into a neighborhood in 1884, they had no way of knowing it would end up being one of Austin's biggest party districts over a century later. Though the original Rainey houses were built between 1885 and 1937, a devastating flood wiped most of them out in 1935 and many residents fled for the suburbs. By the 1950s, a new wave of Hispanic residents inhabited the bungalows on what was a quiet residential street until a 2005 rezoning allowed for commercial development. The real transformation began in 2009 when Bridget Dunlap converted a 1930s-era home into a bar, naming it Lustre Pearl. Other bar entrepreneurs followed suit, and longtime residents began selling their properties and vacating the neighborhood, which had become a rowdy bar district seemingly overnight.

Rainey Street quickly gained national attention, drawing bachelorettes and party-seekers from all over to experience the "charming old houses" that had been converted into bars with food trucks. Revelers line up outside venues and spill out into the street. But now Rainey is going through another transformation. Many of the neighborhood's remaining bungalows have been renovated beyond recognition, turned into modern, multi-level establishments. Even Lustre Pearl, the bar that started it all, is in an entirely different building, while the original bungalow has been moved to the eastside. Others have been torn down and replaced with luxury condos and apartments, which now tower on both sides of the small street. And if the constant cranes and excavators are any indication, there is still more development in the works.

Generally speaking, Rainey Street is where the 6th Street crowd goes once they're slightly older and have more money to spend, so adjust your expectations accordingly. That being said, there are some outliers well-worth a visit if you find yourself in the area. Emmer and Rye, one of the city's top restaurants, is tucked further down, in the south end of the street. Banger's is the only true beer garden in downtown proper. Half Step Bar (page 238) is a sure bet for expertly crafted cocktails, and Little Brother (page 241) seems to be trolling the entire street with its mere existence.

HALF STEP

75½ Rainey Street
Austin, TX 78701

"This is the only bar on Rainey Street I'll step foot into," I hear a voice say behind me. It is a busy Thursday night and we are plastered up against the bar a couple rows deep, watching the bartenders work their magic. This certainly isn't the fastest place on the street to get a drink, but it is, by and large, the best.

Bar veteran Chris Bostick opened Half Step in 2014 with several partners, including cocktail pioneers Eric Alperin

and the late Sasha Petraske. All the partners contributed to the menu development and training as well as the renovation and interior design of the robin's egg blue bungalow. Half Step draws from multiple aesthetics, spanning old Los Angeles and New York to New Orleans and Texas, and much of the functionality of the bar program stems from legendary bars Milk & Honey in New York and The Varnish in LA. The Grateful Dead song "Mississippi Half-Step Uptown Toodleloo"—as well the street address, 75½ Rainey Street—served as inspiration for the name of this music-worshiping cocktail destination.

The bar's interior is upscale—but not overstated—with an undeniably classic feel. Art Deco-inspired light fixtures complement timeless white hex tile and gold floral wallpaper. The interior wood was reclaimed from a friend's house up the street, darkened with stain and char, then warmed up with big velvet curtains. Booth seating in the "living room" area of the house provides a perfectly dark and cozy spot to enjoy the Tuesday night resident Michael Hale Trio or just savor your cocktail undisturbed. As the pink neon sign on the porch reads: "you earned it."

Bostick ran operations until 2016, when the bar was incorporated with Pouring with Heart, a hospitality group that runs top notch bars in California, Colorado, and Texas, including King Bee (see page 92). Half Step breeds some of the best bartenders in town who craft pristine cocktails with none of the pretense. They carve their own ice in-house and draw from a wide library of classics, modern classics, and original creations, while an outdoor bar serves faster batched cocktails for easy access to the outdoor tables.

"Half Step exemplifies the idea of highbrow-lowbrow," says Pouring for Heart director of operations Steven Robbins. "The beauty of Half Step's program is that the same attention to detail is paid to a gin fizz as is to a vodka soda."

BULLDOG COOLER

The Bulldog Cooler is a classic cocktail that can be cloyingly sweet, but lead bartender Cameron Scott revamped it in 2017, adding citrus and fresh ginger syrup to create a refreshing, balanced patio pounder. A very sudden illness unexpectedly took Scott in 2020, a shocking tragedy for the bar community. Half Step celebrates his life with a Cam Jam music showcase and huge party every year on his birthday.

"Cameron was everyone's favorite and one of the best friends I've ever had. He became such an integral part of the bar and quickly developed his craft to become a truly great bartender. He had an effortless talent for making everyone feel welcome, like they were the only one that mattered at the moment, even when we were four deep in the wells. Cameron always treated people with kindness and empathy, as well as keeping close attention to detail. He never stopped learning and trying to make everything better around him. We were in a true golden age at the time Cameron was around and, as lead bartender, he was going to take over as GM at King Bee. He will always be a huge part of our bars as well as many others. We'll never stop missing Cameron." —Steven Robbins, Pouring with Heart's director of operations

2 oz. London dry gin

½ oz. ginger syrup (Half Step uses housemade but Liber & Co brand is a great substitute)

½ oz. fresh orange juice

½ oz. fresh lemon juice

½ oz. fresh pineapple juice

Candied ginger, to garnish

Pineapple chunk, to garnish

1. Whip shake all the ingredients with a small amount of crushed ice, then strain over ice into a Collins glass.
2. Top with soda and garnish with the candied ginger and pineapple chunk.

LITTLE BROTHER

89 Rainey Street
Austin, TX 78701

The Camden Rainey apartments now stand where Lustre Pearl, Rainey's first converted bar, used to. And the building's best amenity by far is Little Brother, a tiny, standing-room only bar on its ground level. When Matthew Bolick, a partner in Wright Bros. Brew & Brew, Better Half Coffee & Cocktails, and Hold Out Brewing, came across the opportunity to open up a concept in the 367-square foot space, he jumped on it.

"It wasn't about the street at all, but about the potential for what we could do in the tiny space," says Bolick, whose very first venture involved selling coffee out of the back of a tiny eastside bookstore. "I thought it sounded hilarious and it immediately made me think of the first Flat Track Coffee and the community that ended up coming out of such a small space."

Bolick's original idea was to do a concept with good coffee, craft beer, natural wine, and "a very nice and professional vibe." But once they decided on the name Little Brother, the bar started to take on a life of its own. When it opened at the start of 2019, the tiny space was already packed with personality. Bolick's childhood TV plays BMX videos in the corner next to a vintage Welcome to Marijuana Country poster, and shelves are stocked with VHS tapes and the Micro Machines of his

youth. One of the first sold-out merch releases included T-shirts declaring Little Brother "the best bar on the worst street."

"We would joke about the business model being Capture the Chad," laughs Bolick. "You've got bros on the street and they're going to roll in regardless, so we could kind of do...whatever?"

They started off hosting "Shitty Brunch" specials, featuring "trash browns" and "Sunny D'mosas." Bar manager Jake Deiotte crafts Zombie Jello shots, Malort boilermakers, and "jammer size" Orange Julius snaquiris. One year in, they opened a truck called Bummer Burrito, just before the city went into lockdown during the pandemic. Next, Bolick launched Bad Larry's Burgers, a smash burger pop-up with an irreverent Instagram account and an immediate cult following, and began delivering the burgers via a hands-free chute on Little Brother's patio. Once the world started opening back up again, he decided to throw a burger party and use the bar's comically small patio as a stage for Rickshaw Billie's Burger Patrol.

"People were finally getting vaccinated and we were so excited about that, we kinda just wanted to shotgun a beer and hug a friend," remembers Bolick. "Turns out that was the start of something much bigger than what we knew it was going to be." Little Brother very quickly became an industry hangout and a most unexpected "venue" for loud punk shows. I found myself there one sunny Monday afternoon, watching in wonder as Deaf Club and Converge thrashed away for a sizable crowd of fans spilling out onto the sidewalk and street for the "secret" show.

"Most of the people there for that show had never been to Rainey Street before. We do have a hardcore crew of regulars though," says Bollick. "If you're a regular at Little Brother, you're the most hardcore regular."

More Locally Loved Rainey Street Bars and Breweries:

THE DRAFTING ROOM
88½ Rainey Street, Austin, TX 78701

THE STAGGER LEE
87 Rainey Street, Austin, TX 78701

BANGER'S SAUSAGE HOUSE & BEER GARDEN
79 Rainey Street, Austin, TX 78701

THE STAY PUT
73 Rainey Street, Austin, TX 78701

EAST CÉSAR CHÁVEZ AND HOLLY

The stretch of East César Chávez Street between I-35 and Chicon Street is hugged on the east by the Holly neighborhood, which spans from Chicon to Pleasant Valley. The northern boundary for both neighborhoods is East 7th Street, and Festival Beach forms the southern border. César Chávez, which is appropriately named after the civil rights activist and labor leader who fought for farm workers, initially cut through farmland. It was then subdivided and sold to World War I veterans, who went on to build many of the original bungalows in the early 1900s.

Mexican-Americans settled in this neighborhood after World War II, as the city pushed its residents of color east of downtown. The César Chávez and Holly neighborhoods consisted of primarily Latino residents, and their businesses and churches, for a number of years. In 1999, the city adopted a new "Neighborhood Plan" that promoted mixed-use development. Large residential buildings started to rise, with the cost of living and property taxes, along César Chávez. Like much of East Austin, these neighborhoods are a contrasting mix of the original bungalows and large modern townhomes and duplexes, often one right next to the other. There are a few remaining ornate Victorian homes along César Chávez, as well as some Craftsman-style bungalows, most of which have been turned into offices and businesses. In the last decade, the street has filled up with coffee shops, breweries, art studios, bike shops, yoga studios, and venues, plus restaurants like Oseyo, Sushi Bar, Intero, and Ezov. Though gentrification has drastically changed the neighborhood, long-standing restaurants like Juan in a Million, which opened in 1980, and Mr. Natural, which opened in 1988, have stood the test of time, along with a number of family-run piñata shops and taquerias. This is also one of the more colorful parts of Austin, where walls are splashed with murals celebrating the city's Chicano heritage.

DRINKS LOUNGE & RECORDS

2001 E César Chávez Street
Austin, TX 78702

Tim and Sara Lupa know a thing or two about running a long-lasting neighborhood watering hole; they've been working in bars for most of their adult lives— she as a bartender and he as support staff. When Tim came across the opportunity to buy The Brixton in 2009, they quit their main jobs and took a chance that had them running the punk rock dive for the next 10 years.

When the owner of Big D's, a sports bar on César Chávez decided to retire, Tim worked out a deal to buy the spacious bar on the corner of César Chávez and Lynn Street. Originally built in 1942, it was a Chinese grocery store called Tak-Hom Foods before it was a liquor store in the 1960s and then a number of different Tejano bars through the years. Since 2014, Drinks Lounge & Records has been a staple of the Holly neighborhood. Drive by on any given night and the Astroturfed patio out front is usually filled with friends and the bike rack around the perimeter lined with bikes.

"We just wanted to create a place where everyone felt welcome to hang out," says Tim. "It was mostly locals

when we first opened. These days it's a mixture of locals, AirBnB tourists, and people exploring the east side."

The distinct blue building opens up via garage door to a spacious, dark interior with a horseshoe bar, high-top tables, and two pool tables. Big black booths run down one side, with black and white photos of musicians watching over each: Lemmy and Phil "Philthy Animal" Taylor from Motörhead, The Ramones, The Sex Pistols, Iggy Pop, and Debbie Harry.

The bar menu features a rotating list of signature cocktails like Como La Flor—Still Austin Gin, Martine honeysuckle, and grapefruit—and Hot Love—ghost pepper tequila, jalapeño, lime, agave, and Tajín. There's also classic cocktails, draught and canned beer, zero-proof creations, and always a couple of frozen options. And Drinks always manages to keep their prices beyond reasonable for this neighborhood, with most cocktails running $9-$12. They also serve food until midnight each night, with incredible deals on different days of the week. Mondays are industry night with half-price burgers and free pool. On Taco Tuesday, tacos are just $2, and Wednesdays are for half-price wings.

"Back in the day, we used to be able to do $1 Lone Star beer, but these days we can't even buy them for $1," says Tim. "Add in rising property taxes, rent never goes down, and we started providing health insurance for our crew. We feel it's a very delicate balance of taking care of everyone, customers and crew."

If the records hung on the wall behind the bar are any indication, music is a huge part of the program at Drinks. DJs spin every weekend, including DJ When I Feel Like It aka Tim Lupa. They're constantly throwing themed dance parties, from Selena to Prince, plus Karaoke Underground events and fundraisers for neighborhood causes and Austin charities. In February 2022, they opened a record store inside the bar, too, so now they host new release listening parties and in-store performances, called Drinks Sessions, that are recorded and added to the Drinks Records YouTube channel.

BUFALINA

2215 E César Chávez Street
Austin, TX 78702

It was wine that first stole Steven Dilley's heart. His downtown brokerage firm was around the corner from The Austin Wine Merchant, so he began regularly picking up bottles after work and slowly expanding his knowledge. Next, a trading career led the native Texan up to New York, where he was exposed to incredible pizza at a time when Neapolitan pies were starting to explode in popularity. After eight years, he felt like a career change was in order, and moved back to Austin. He wanted to open a restaurant, but his experience was limited to his own home kitchen experiments. So he spent time in Naples, learning to make pizza at different places, before returning to seek out the perfect space for his wine and pizza concept. In July 2013, he opened an intimate wine bar and restaurant in a former engine shop on César Chávez.

Bufalina was an immediate success, and for good reason. For one, the pizza is some of the best in town, made with a fermented dough that is fired to perfection—with just the right amount of chew and char—in a white-tiled Stefano Ferrara oven. The simple menu featured about a half dozen different Neapolitan pies, plus salads and other fresh, seasonal sides and starters like housemade mozzarella and stracciatella plates. The dessert offering was a simple vanilla ice cream drizzled with sherry. But Bufalina started to garner just as much praise for its wine program, which leaned toward low intervention, small production bottles made with lesser-known grape varieties. When Dilley decided to expand to a second location on Burnet Road, he brought on Rania Zayyat, an Advanced Sommelier with experience working at top restaurants in Houston and Austin. Zayyat helped develop the wine program for the new restaurant, then worked her way from general manager to wine director to partner. The wine program has now grown to over 700 selections, with the concentration of them produced in France, northern Italy, Spain, Catalunya, and the US, plus some selections from Germany, Eastern Europe, Mexico, and Chile. In 2020, they launched a monthly wine club as a way to support their importers and supplies during the pandemic.

"Our wine program is a collection of winegrowers and winemakers who believe in growing, fermenting, and producing wines using natural methods, while prioritizing the human and environmental impacts of their businesses," explains Zayyat, who cites Megan Bell and Pierre Gonon Chasselas as two of her current favorite producers. "We celebrate pioneering producers along with rising stars, and strive to make our program accessible and fun." She recalls finding inspiration in the first location of Terroir in New York, where the serious wine list was presented in a Trapper Keeper full of fun tidbits, notes, and doodles. In the same unpretentious spirit, Bufalina's massive wine list is printed on regular printer paper and stapled. All wines are poured into the same all-purpose glasses and Erlenmeyer flasks serve as decanters. And when you ask for the check, it comes inside a vintage paperback.

In February 2021, Bufalina had to move out of their building because it was set to be demolished to make way for a new development. Dilley was able to secure an old laundromat, just a half mile further east on César Chávez, and reopen by November 2022. The space, which is only slightly bigger than the original, has been flawlessly replicated, with the same farmhouse-style wooden tables, simple votives, Edison pendant bulbs, and an open kitchen design offering a good view of the action around the wood-burning oven. In another delicious plot twist, Dilley brought on chef Grae Nonas (formerly of Olamaie and Le Cowboy), who's fine-tuned an incredible house-made pasta program for the expanded dinner menu.

I was happy to learn that their steal of a daily happy hour deal—50 percent off pies and bottles under $100 from 4:00 to 5:30 p.m. —carried through to the new location. And so did their first come, first served seating policy. It means you're almost always going to have to wait, either on the benches outside or at the wine bar if you can snag a seat, but it's the perfect excuse to drink a little extra wine and get excited for the incredible meal you're about to enjoy.

More Locally Loved César Chávez and Holly Bars and Breweries:

HISTORIC SCOOT INN
1308 E 4th Street, Austin, TX 78702

LOU'S EASTSIDE
1900 E César Chávez Street, Austin, TX 78702

THE CORAL SNAKE
1910 E César Chávez Street, Austin, TX 78702

HIGH NOON
2000 E César Chávez Street, Austin, TX 78702

BUCKET'S SPORTS BAR
2020 E César Chávez Street, Austin, TX 78702

LOVEBIRDS
2337 E César Chávez Street, Austin, TX 78702

BLUE OWL BREWING
2400 E César Chávez Street, #300, Austin, TX 78702

KEMURI TATSU-YA
2713 E 2nd Street, Austin, TX 78702

SOUTH SHORE, RIVERSIDE, AND MONTOPOLIS

Riverside Drive runs parallel to Lady Bird Lake, which is not actually a lake but a section of the Colorado River. It winds past Auditorium Shores, with a beautiful view of the skyline, then passes South Congress and takes you through the green Travis Heights neighborhood. But once you pass I-35 and it becomes East Riverside, the street changes discernibly. It's basically a corridor of strip mall after strip mall punctuated with fast food and taquerias; Rosita's Al Pastor and Taco More are two favorites.

The cross streets of Wickersham and Grove both lead to a network of massive apartment complexes that are popular with students and lower-income residents. But East Riverside started changing when the first new developments went up right next to I-35 around 2011, and the sprawling South Shore development followed soon after in 2013, bringing with it a handful of modern fast-casual restaurants like Mour Cafe, Chi'Lantro, and Pho Please, plus a big new Walgreens and an urgent care. Then in 2018, Oracle rolled out a 27-acre campus on South Lake Shore Boulevard, displacing many longtime residents in the process.

There are two venues on East Riverside, Emo's East and Come and Take It Live, and Club Carnaval has been packing their dance floor since 1987. There aren't a ton of bars in the area at the moment, but that will undoubtedly change over the next few years. Right now, everything is pretty far apart and this part of Riverside isn't particularly walkable. That being said, the bars I've highlighted here are just the kind of community spaces needed for a neighborhood in flux. The Buzz Mill was one of the first to open, in 2013, with the goal of cultivating community. The 24-hour coffee shop and bar organizes river clean-ups, and hosts workshops in survival skills. Pass over Montopolis and you'll reach Ani's Day & Night (page 258), an all-day cafe and bar set on keeping prices reasonable and welcoming neighbors into its spacious yard as if it was their own. And both bars act as incubators for food trucks, in a city where it is increasingly hard for mobile vendors to find a place to park.

ANI'S DAY & NIGHT

7107 E Riverside Drive
Austin, TX 78741

Once you pass Grove Boulevard, while heading east on Riverside, the traffic thins out a bit and the street becomes a little greener and calmer. On your right, you'll see a cheery white and lime green house, its front yard draped with twinkling lights. Is that some sort of a party? Why, yes it is, and you're invited.

Freddy Fernandez grew up in this 1930s-era Victorian home in the late 1970s, with his parents and six siblings, back when the Montopolis neighborhood was nothing but farmland. Though his family left the property in 1999, Fernandez was able to buy it back in 2001 as a gift for his mother, who suggested he transform it into a business. That's how it became the first Fast Freddy's Hair Salon and, although he closed this location in 2019, others remain open.

Service industry veteran Rachael Garbowski was seeking out a space to open a bar concept, when she found out about the East Riverside property through a friend of a friend. She fell in love with the house and approached Fernandez with an idea to lease the space and honor the Fernandez family legacy with an all-day cafe and bar named after his mother, Aniceta "Cheta" Limon. Limon was born in 1930 and spent her whole life in Austin. She is remembered by her family and friends for her excellent cooking, her love of dancing and throwing parties, and her entrepreneurial spirit. When Ani's opened in May 2021, a portrait of the eponymous monarch, created by artist Sam Sanford, was hung on the wall in her honor.

While converting the historic home into a bar space, Garbowski wanted to be sure to honor its unique architecture, seen in the high ceilings, tall windows, wood floors and original shiplap. She brought in Kathleen Rubin of Room is Blue to create a design that playfully combines classic and contemporary elements. Many of the original furniture and fixtures maintained by the Fernandez family are still in place, from the hallway chandelier to a red velvet couch. The white-washed walls

of the interior are the perfect canvas for work by local artists—and have served as a backdrop for photo shoots and music videos too. The front of the cement-top bar, as well as the wall behind the bar, has been laid with green tiles that match the porch floor and stairs. The front window trim is painted a brighter green, with daffodil yellow accents, and matching picnic tables are laid out across the spacious front yard, which is kid- and dog-friendly—there's even leash hooks on the tables!

Ani's coffee program uses locally roasted beans from Greater Goods and features a variety of unique coffee creations—like the Peaches 'n' Cream, made with espresso, milk, peach simple syrup, peach bitters and dried peach—as well as your standard drip coffee and espresso drinks. There is local, craft beer on tap, but you can also opt for a $3 Lone Star or Coors Banquet. Garbowski also curates an all-natural wine list, and keeps those selections reasonably priced too. They feature a couple of more classic draft cocktails, plus a menu of punny originals like Live and Let Rye, Tequila Me Softly and Better Call Mezcal. Aperol We've Been Through, their most popular frozen, even inspired a mural on the back of the building.

Ani's doesn't serve food, but instead provides a home to food trucks like Nyam Sunshine Cuisine, Las Alegres Comadres, and The Forking Vegan. Garbowski also hosts various food-centric events and pop-ups, so there is almost always something different to taste here. More often than not, the yard is buzzing with activity, whether it's because of a fundraiser, yard sale, live music, clothing swap, art market, DJ-fueled dance party, spring crawfish boil, or winter s'mores roast over the fire pits. Garbowski—who has worked in development for the Contemporary Austin, Big Medium and the Texas Land Conservancy—also hosts space for artists to share their work with the community, an invaluable opportunity in a city where studio and gallery spaces are getting harder to secure.

"This project is distinctly Austin in many ways, with a little something for everyone," Garbowski explains. "It's for the neighborhood. It's unpretentious. It's indoor-outdoor. It's simple and straightforward. We are dedicated to preserving the character of the original house, keeping green space, and truly serving our neighbors."

...BABY, ONE MORE LIME

It's hard to avoid tequila in this city, but it usually appears in the form of a Margarita or a Ranch Water. This creation is a little different and unexpected, just like the Austin you've read about. It's creamy and bright, with herbs and spice— just perfect for sipping on Ani's patio in the springtime.

1½ oz. tequila

½ oz. Strega

1 oz. coconut cream

1 oz. fresh lime juice

½ oz. Thai Chili Agave

Dried lime, to garnish

Tajín, to garnish

1. Shake all ingredients together in a cocktail tin filled with ice.

2. Strain over ice (preferably crushed ice) into a highball of fresh ice.

3. Garnish with dried lime and a sprinkle of Tajín.

Thai Chili Agave: Stir equal parts agave and near-boiling hot water in a quart container until dissolved. Add 2-3 dried Thai chilis and let steep at least 24 hours before fine straining. For extra heat, break up the chilis before adding to the agave syrup, but be sure not to touch your eyes or face!

FRAZIER'S LONG & LOW

2538 Elmont Drive
Austin, TX 78741

After seeing great success with White Horse (page 144), Nathan Hill partnered with his general manager, hospitality veteran Michael Frazier, on a project just south of the river. Frazier's Long & Low opened in February 2019, tucked just south of East Riverside, on the corner of Pleasant Valley and Elmont Drive.

"Frazier's is a 1970s truck stop diner that was loved and kept more or less clean over the decades," says Hill. "It's your cool uncle's basement bar. It's a no-frills, pretension-free bar that invites you to belly up next to a stranger for hours on end 'til the lights turn up."

If not for the flat screen TVs against the wood-paneled walls behind the dark mahogany bar, you might actually think you stumbled back into the late 1970s. Dark blue ceiling tiles, dark brown floor tiles, leather bar stools, and rounded booths create a cozy, retro vibe. Pops of color come from red vintage Coors lamps about the pool tables and colorful stained glass Schlitz lamps above the shuffleboard, plus goldenrod-felted pool tables to match the heavy curtains. Hill's collection of vintage beer signs is displayed all over the bar, and even the old-school Starlight jukebox leans heavy into vintage albums, from Charles Bradley to Townes Van Zandt and Black Sabbath.

The side walls are covered in blue, gold, and brown patterned wallpaper that, upon closer look, you'll notice has a Basset hound head incorporated into its design. There's also a hound profiled on the yellow board outside the dog-friendly patio. That's because Frazier's Bassett hounds are what inspired the "Long & Low" part of the name. "But it also has a life message built in," discloses Hill. "Long life, low stress."

Even the food menu is straight out of the 1970s, featuring bar food favorites like chopped cheese, fried pickle spears, patty melts, chili dogs and corn dogs, served every day from noon until 2am. There are some simple cocktails, like a spicy Paloma and a lavender lemonade spiked with Tito's vodka or Still gin. And you never know

what color the day's Jello shots might be. There are also a number of crafty local taps—and a shelf displaying the canned beer selections alongside trophies, a bowling pin and a football helmet—but Coors Banquet, poured into a frosty mug, is the brew of choice. In fact, Frazier's is one of the nation's top sellers of Coors, with only Colorado's Coors Field and Red Rocks Amphitheatre surpassing them in sales. "We're kind of a big deal," says Hill. "And Frazier's $2 Coors on Thursday is a big hit. Like a $1.50 hot dog at Costco, it will never change." The bar's signature Long and Low combo is a Coors Banquet and a shot of whiskey for just $6.

You know that idea of Austin people form after they watch the movie *Dazed & Confused*? That version of Austin, which is long gone in real life, has been captured inside Frazier's. I feel like Matthew McConaughey would feel right at home here. Hell, he'd probably share his fries with you. And if he showed up during Frazier's annual 420 party, he'd win the joint rolling competition too.

But if cowboys hats, which the staff don every Friday, and tattoos aren't your thing, that's okay. "Everyone is welcome, as long as you behave," says Hill. "Or reasonably misbehave."

THE JACKALOPE SOUTH SHORE

1523 Tinnin Ford Road
Austin, TX 78741

Native Austinite Jason Burton grew up in the city's bar and music industry, opening and managing bars that were instrumental to the Red River scene in the early 1990s and aughts, like Stubb's, Club de Ville, and Ocean's 11. Then he did something risky: he saved up all his tips and took a gamble on opening his own bar on 6th Street in 2004.

"Lots of nights, my dog and I were the only employees," remembers Burton. "[It was a] big risk because all the cool kids were hanging on Red River, but it worked out!"

He opened the original Jackalope location in one of the oldest buildings in Austin— and one of the first to become a licensed bar in the 1800s. The bar's theme was inspired by a jackalope tattoo he has, "and a love of legendary beasts of the night," he says. On a street filled with bars catered more toward tourists and co-eds, The Jackalope intrigued with its dark edginess: black velvet paintings of topless girls, a bestickered back patio screening B-movies to a punk soundtrack, and a giant jackalope statue just asking to be straddled for a photo. They also became well-known for their cider-based sake bombs, giant tropical Helldorado cocktails—served with a handful of glowing straws so you can share with friends—and way better burgers and wings than you'd expect to find at a divey bar on 6th Street. In fact, at one point The Food Network named theirs the "Best Burger Ever."

After years of continued success downtown, Burton renovated an old 1970s country dance club off East Riverside and opened a new rendition of The Jackalope in 2016. This location is massive, with four red-felted pool tables instead of just one. There's disco balls and pin-up art, glittering gold tabletops that emulate the OG Jackalope's bar top, and variegated shiplap takes the place of historic stone walls. And South Shore has its own giant

DRINK LIKE A LOCAL: AUSTIN

jackalope too. This one is an outdoor enthusiast, geared out with a camping pack, lantern and canteen—and even has steps to help you climb into its saddle.

It's also very different from the original—but then again, so is Austin. The massive bar is lined with TVs, and they're playing sports instead of cult movies. It also shares an expansive yard with the adjacent Copperhead Club that seems built for the masses moving to South Shore. The dog-friendly space is filled with picnic tables and surrounded by colorful murals, with cornhole and giant Jenga. They also use the space to host a variety of fun events: a Dachshund dash on Derby Day, an adult Easter egg hunt, water balloon fights, steak nights.

Of course, you can find Jackalope's now-famous burgers at the South Shore location too, with toppings ranging from BBQ pulled pork with spicy slaw to chipotle pimento cheese with bacon and pickles—plus waffle fries, sweet potato tots, buffalo cauliflower, and more. This bar also has a greater focus on local drafts, as well as craft cocktails that rotate regularly, like the Paloma-inspired Smoke and Mirrors, made with El Silencio Mezcal, Aperol, lime, and Jarritos grapefruit soda.

These days, the original Jackalope has a few remnants from its punk past, but you'll typically hear hip hop blasting for the Dirty 6th crowd that has taken over. "Downtown is in a stage of being mostly a nighttime party bar, with DJ's," says Burton. "Jackalope South Shore is more what the old place used to be, with the artists, musicians, and service industry crowd. Downtown is now a very high energy, young crowd, whereas South Shore is a bit more laidback scene. We have always strived to be a bar that appeals to anyone who wants to get aboard, and not be defined by a particular crowd or scene. As Austin has changed, so have the bars."

ISLAND CAMPER

The Island Camper has been on Jackalope's drink menu from the very first day the downtown location opened, and it hasn't left since. It is an old island recipe Burton encountered while visiting some of his rum producers in the Caribbean.

1 oz. Mount Gay 8-year-old rum

1½ oz. Sugar Island Coconut Rum

Crushed fresh ginger

Raspberry Hibiscus Tea (to volume)

1 splash fresh lime juice

Hibiscus, to garnish

Lime wedge, to garnish

1. Add ingredients to a tin with ice and shake vigorously to infuse the ginger.
2. Strain into a tall glass filled with ice, garnished with a fresh lime wedge and a hibiscus flower.

Raspberry Hibiscus Tea: Boil 1 gallon water, pour over 1 cup dried hibiscus leaves, and let brew for 10 minutes. Strain and add 1 cup fresh pureed raspberries. Chill for 24 hours.

WHIP IN

1950 S I-35 Frontage Road
Austin, TX 78704

If you weren't looking for Whip In, you might just drive right past it on the southbound feeder of I-35. After all, it could easily be mistaken for any of the other convenience stores along the highway between East Riverside and Oltorf. That's because Whip In started out as one too, opened in 1986 by Indian immigrants Amrit and Chandan Topiwala. When they started to stock their fridge with imported beers, they attracted a following for their unique curation, which stood out from all the other quickie marts in town. When beer sales surpassed gas sales, they removed the gas tanks from the front of the store, then started paring down the groceries and essentials lining their shelves, focusing instead on their beer and wine selection. When their son Dipak returned home from the West Coast with his family to manage the store in the early aughts, he introduced a food program. It began with simple "panaani" wraps, but soon grew to include Tex-Mex/Indian mash-ups, like a chutney queso, plus nutritious Gujarati curries and stews made using his mom's recipes and local ingredients.

Whip In has taken many forms over the last twenty years. Dipak introduced a tiny stage and used church pews, vintage tables, carved wooden screens, and Indian tapestries to create a DIY venue while the space was still part convenience store. They hosted live music, trivia, and indie filming screens. The walls were decked with Hindu artwork and Indian beer signs, and there was always some Nag Champa wafting through the

air. Then it transformed into a full-fledged gastropub with 72 taps, a full kitchen, and hand-written chalkboards displaying the offerings above the bar. The stage became bigger and they built another stage outside in a courtyard filled with picnic tables. For a period of time, Whip In was a microbrewery too, crafting small batches of lager and ale made to accompany their dishes. And at one point, there was a separate wine bar inside the space, as they ramped up their wine program and started to include more small production wines made without additives.

Zahir Prasla, who owns Quickie Pickie, a historic convenience store he modernized, bought the business from Topiwala in 2017 and remodeled the inside. When you enter now, you're greeted with a section of wine from around the world and coolers filled with packaged beer from breweries like Equal Parts Brewing, Dutchess Ales, Burlington Beer, Jester King, Bear King Brewing, Real Ale Brewing Co, and Family Business Beer Company. The original bar now stretches across the back of the building, featuring 95 taps and a large grid menu behind the bar describes which beer, wine, or kombucha is flowing from each one. The menu is bigger than ever, offering snacks like masala wings and lamb samosas, plus entire sections of tandoor items, curries, wraps, biryanis, rice, and even noodles; while the Whip In of the past was inspired by truck stop dhabas, this version is influenced by British curry pubs. The dining room is now filled with high tops, bar stools, and one longer table, situated in front of a new and improved stage. Along the side, light wooden booths with slanted backs have been installed, and each nook is decorated with a poster from one of Whip In's early shows, a reminder of that bar's scrappy, but soulful, past.

More Locally Loved South Shore and Riverside Bars:

COPPERHEAD CLUB
2120 E Riverside Drive, Austin, TX 78741

EMO'S EAST
2015 E Riverside Drive, Austin, TX 78741

COME AND TAKE IT LIVE
2015 E Riverside Drive, Building 4, Austin, TX 78741

THE BUZZ MILL
1505 Town Creek Drive, Austin, TX 78741

SOUTH LAMAR AND SOUTH 1ST STREET

Lamar Boulevard is the main artery that runs through the city, changing from North to South as it crosses Lady Bird Lake. This is where West Riverside Drive begins, running parallel to the Colorado River as it cuts through Auditorium Shores. A beautiful city skyline backdrop has made this park a popular site for many festivals and events throughout the year. South Lamar then hits Barton Springs Road, which will lead you to Zilker Park if you head west on it. The metropolitan park boasts 351 acres of green space, including Barton Springs, a large, spring-fed pool that remains a cool 68 degrees through the year. Zilker Park is also the site of many events—most notably Austin City Limits, a music festival that takes place across two weekends each October. As you continue further south on Lamar Boulevard, you'll encounter most of the bars listed in this section, as well as a number of restaurants, like Uchi, Loro, Odd Duck, and Matt's El Rancho. Due to its proximity to downtown, this thoroughfare has seen some significant development in the last decade, with more in the works. South Lamar is now lined with towering mixed-use high-rises, which has made the road slightly more walkable, but has also significantly increased traffic.

If you head east on Barton Springs from Lamar, you'll come to South 1st Street, where in 1970 music pioneer Eddie Wilson opened the legendary Armadillo World Headquarters. The venue ignited Austin's psychedelic and outlaw country music scene, led by Willie Nelson, and helped solidify the city as the "Live Music Capital" it is still known as today. In 1996, Wilson opened up a second location of Threadgill's just a block away on Barton Springs and Riverside. Wilson ran the restaurant and venue until 2018, when soaring rent forced them to shutter. Needless to say, this area of town holds an important place in Austin history. When you climb the hill heading south on South 1st Street, you'll enter the Bouldin Creek neighborhood. Both Zilker and Bouldin Creek are, unsurprisingly, very expensive neighborhoods, where bohemian bungalows reside alongside mammoth modern buildings. South 1st Street is lined with local restaurants like Elizabeth Street Cafe, 1417 French Bistro, Lenoir, and Polvos, plus galleries, shops, murals, and food truck parks. South 1st Street runs parallel to South Lamar and, though it has also seen some changes through the years, it still has an unmistakable old Austin charm about it.

BARTON SPRINGS SALOON

424 S Lamar Boulevard
Austin, TX 78704

They just don't make 'em like Jim LeMond anymore. The mythical barman had the height, dramatic mustache, and captivating tales of a bar world Paul Bunyan. While he might not have really been the first person in Austin, which he loved to tell people with a grin, the native Austinite did grow up here and spun a wide web for himself in the hospitality industry. But he really kickstarted his career by opening The Cloak Room (page 193) in the late 1970s, when he was just 24 years old. He sold it after a couple years and found himself at the Cedar Door, where he went on to become, beyond just a general manager, an absolute fixture of the bar. And he loved that place so much he dedicated over 30 years of his life to working there, and followed it to several locations around the city—that's right, the turn-of-the-century bordello, originally built downtown, was a nomadic bar that moved around the city a total of four times; it even had "Follow That Bar" bumper stickers! When the Cedar Door's owners decided to sell the historic bar, Jim and his wife Rebecca hatched a plan to relocate it to a location on Toomey Road. Barton Springs Road was already home to a number of restaurants, like the flagship Chuy's, Shady Grove, Baby Acapulco, and Green Mesquite BBQ, and yet there wasn't a single bar

in the neighborhood. But while they were working with the owner to secure the necessary zoning to sell mixed beverages, the Cedar Door owner received an offer he couldn't refuse, and sold it to its current owners, who moved it to Brazos and 2nd Streets, where it's stayed ever since.

"Jim really wanted to be able to buy the Cedar Door and keep that legacy going, but unfortunately that was too cost prohibitive," remembers Rebecca. "But it did seren-dipitously lead us to drive past that corner every day."

The corner she refers to is Barton Springs Road and South Lamar, where a long-abandoned Texaco gas station stood. Jim said it had been there as long as he could remember, and discovered it had been empty for seven years, so they set their sights on opening their own bar concept in it. He returned to working behind the bar at the Cedar Door while they spent the next two years jumping through hoops to secure the building for commercial use, remediating the property by removing the gas tanks, and testing the groundwater for contaminants. In May of 2006, Barton Springs Saloon became the first bar to open south of the river on Lamar.

You could see the Cedar Door's inspiration in the bar's dark wooden interior and the mirror behind the back bar. But Barton Springs Saloon was like its rough-around-the-edges country cousin, with mismatched furniture and taxidermy hung on beige-painted cinder block walls. A couple of second-hand couches faced the pool table, with Golden Tee and Buck Hunter in the corner, and a Coors Light sign read "Come in to B.S. & party!" In an area of town that was quickly becoming more commercial, Barton Springs Saloon, in all its no-frills glory, was a place you could always sidle up to the bar and get a highball for just a few dollars—or a beer for even less.

"Austin has changed so much I don't even recognize it," says Rebecca, who moved to Austin from Dallas and put herself through UT by bartending in the 1980s. "If you had told me 20 years ago what we'd be looking at right now, I wouldn't have believed you."

Of course, some evolution has been inevitable for the bar too, but they've made those changes without sacrificing its old school charm. Bar veterans Alan Custer and Alec Mackay came on as managing partners in 2018 and developed a cocktail program to meet the growing demand. Now, their chalkboard menu lists options like Gin & Juice, a mezcal mule made with fresh rosemary, and a margarita made with fresh watermelon juice. The bar has also upgraded to a 23-tap beer wall, featuring craft brew from near and far. But their prices are still some of the most competitive in the neighborhood; in fact, you can still get their famous Lunchbox deal—an ice cold Lonestar and a shot of whiskey—for just $6, which is unheard of anywhere else on Barton Springs Road.

Faux stone accent walls now give the interior a warm lodgey feel, the bathroom went through a much-needed remodel, and the patio's outdoor seating has been greatly expanded. They've cycled through several food trucks through the years but are seeing great success these days with the popular Tommy Want Wingy. On any given night, the awning-covered patio is filled with groups of friends, watching the game, throwing back drinks, snacking on wings—and usually commingling with other groups.

"Although it's still very South Austin, it's a different clientele," says Rebecca. "We've always drawn from the community for our customer base, but now our customer base is coming from condos and people in tech jobs. But we still get biker groups, artists, teachers...Everything around us has changed, but our customer base has always been very diverse." The bar community very sadly lost Jim in 2019, but there is no doubt he would be thrilled to see his bar thriving in an ever-changing Austin, bringing together people from all walks of life. "It's always stayed a neighborhood bar, which is really odd to think about, with all the changes that have gone on around us," says Rebecca. "We're still just the corner neighborhood bar."

TIKI TATSU-YA

1300 S Lamar Boulevard
Austin, TX 78704

In the space next door to Ramen Tatsu-ya's South Lamar location, there's an Aikawa Tropical Tours storefront. "Ask about our travel deals!" the white print on the window exclaims. "Cheap flights!" If the archaic MySpace logo in the window doesn't give them away, the "Gone Surfing" sign will because, here in Austin, we are hundreds of miles from the ocean. However, it sure won't feel like it once you pass under the glowing red buoy suspended in a fishnet over the thatched roof entrance. You have entered Tiki Tatsu-Ya, the immersive tiki bar created by the Tatsu and Shion Aikawa, the brothers behind the Ramen Tatsu-Ya restaurant group.

The team started tossing around ideas for a tiki concept as early as 2014, inspired by bars like Tiki-Ti in Los Angeles and San Francisco's False Idol, Smuggler's Cove, and Tonga Room & Hurricane Bar. They sketched out some ideas but ended up going in a different direction and opened Kemuri Tatsu-Ya on East 2nd Street instead. But when the space next to their South Lamar Ramen Tatsu-Ya location became available in 2018, they dove back into tiki research.

"We went on a pilgrimage to the West coast—on a week-long binge of rum and juice, visiting bars and restaurants and holes, wholesalers of exotic wares—on a mad dash to soak in every detail we could," remembers Shion Aikawa. They bar hopped from San Francisco to Los Angeles to San Diego, found an importer that specialized in tiki decor, and ended the trip at the Tiki Oasis trade show, where they networked and collected more pieces for the bar. When the pandemic hit and the opening date was indefinitely delayed, Shion says they went deeper than ever into their research, adding much more detail to the project than would've been possible under normal circumstances. To call this place simply a "tiki bar" feels like a huge understatement. "It's a tiki bar on acid," says Shion, "Disneyland for tikiphiles."

The team created an entire fictional backstory for the bar, whereby the Aikawa brothers are operating a small travel agency geared toward thrill seekers and surfers on an unnamed Pacific Ocean island. When they discover a cave at the base of a volcano, filled with relics left by the Japanese explorers who found the island in 1619 and a rum distillery they were forced to leave abruptly,

they transform it into a bar tying together elements of Japan, Hawaii, and Polynesia. The recount of this tale plays through speakers in the bathroom while you're immersed in this fantastical world the team created over the course of three years with the help of design studio McCray & Co. and Blue Genie Art Industries.

Two wooden porthole doors lead into a cave filled with a two-story rock fountain shaped like a shisa dragon, a mythological Japanese guardian. The rock walls are lined with skulls, Polynesian masks, and nautical details like fishing nets and floats, and the main wood-carved bar displays a library collection of 250 rums from over 20 countries. On the second level, the Ama-San table honors Japanese pearl divers, and the shibori-lined Fugu Hut is decorated with bamboo ceilings hung with pufferfish. Downstairs, the Captain's Hull booth depicts the ancient trade ship that discovered the island, while another space pays respect to the forefathers of tiki with a collection of mugs, ashtrays, matchbooks, and swizzle sticks dating back to the 1930s.

The drinks are mainly homages to classic tiki cocktails and the menu takes the form of a fold-out map detailing the story behind each one. "What we try to do is make the best version of these drinks as possible, while also including some unique ingredients not necessarily in the originals, not to change the drink but enhance it," explains beverage manager Cory Starr, who moved to Austin from Chicago, where he worked at the renowned Three Dots and a Dash.

For example, their take on a Mai Tai uses miso orgeat, and substitutes mandarin for curaçao, and their spin on the lesser-known brandy-and-gin-based Suffering Bastard is amped up with shōchū, Cynar, and ume plum shrub. Each drink comes in a custom-designed vessel, and their shareable, large drinks are next-level. The looming Skeleton Cruise—made with Japanese whisky, rum, Chartreuse, guava, lemon, pineapple, and pomegranate—comes on a ship adorned with skulls and gold chocolate coins and seeping with fog, and the S.O.S.

Stranded is served in a smoky orb filled with shōchū, starfruit, passionfruit, miso-almond orgeat, and phol-ernum, the bar's own falernum recipe made with added pho spices.

A surf and exotica soundtrack commingles with ambient sounds like trickling water and birds cawing, interrupted every now and then by a tropical storm. And the Hawaiian-inspired food menu features dishes like loco moco, seaweed salad, poke, musubi, and a pu-pu platter loaded with BBQ beef skewers, mochiko wings, taro tots, and more. You'll leave feeling like the most satisfied castaway to ever wash up on shore.

THE BROKEN SPOKE

3201 S Lamar Boulevard
Austin, TX 78704

There's arguably no more iconic Austin bar than The Broken Spoke. A visit to The Tourist Trap will leave no doubt in your mind about that. The little DIY museum tucked in the side of the legendary honky-tonk is laden with Texas history in the form of old show posters, menus, album covers, signs, and newspaper articles. The walls are covered with framed photos of founder James White, in his signature rhinestones and fringe, posing alongside the many country stars who have graced its stage, from Ernest Tubb and Jerry Jeff Walker to Dolly Parton and Garth Brooks. Glass display cases are filled with artifacts: a cigar butt smoked by Bob Wills, Willie Nelson's bandanna, antique cowboys boots and spurs, and an entire collection of cowboy hats donated by Ray Benson, Marty Stuart, Sammy Allred—even Lyndon B. Johnson.

The Broken Spoke was dreamt up by 8th generation Austinite James White while he was stationed overseas in the army. And when the 25-year-old returned home in 1964, he made that dream a reality. Working with sparse funds and relying on the manpower of his stepdad, friends, and community volunteers, they built the bar and cafe from the ground up. "It was the middle of nowhere back then," recalls Stephanie Crow, who's worked here for 45 years. "All there was was that oak tree and a two-lane highway. We had to funnel in water from a horse farm nearby!"

By the next year, they added on the dancehall and bandstand to accommodate growing demand, began hosting live music five days a week, and haven't stopped since. Each Tuesday through Thursday, two-steppers glide in loops across the concrete slab dancefloor, flanked on both sides by tables with red-checkered tablecloths and glowing neon beer signs. White would only hire people that could play two-step, and to this day the honky-tonk bears a sign on the dancefloor warning "No Line Dancing! All Violators will be sent back to California!" If it reads like a joke, it's not: line dancing disrupts the counterclockwise flow of two stepping. There's another strict rule: no halter or tank tops. As James used to say, "This is not a swimming pool." Eighty-year-old Annetta, his wife of 58 years, still works the bar on weekends, and she will not think twice about kicking out a tank top.

"She's meaner than the day is long but she's got a beautiful heart!" says Stephanie with a smile.

James passed away in January of 2021, but the Spoke remains a family affair. His daughter Ginny hires bands and handles PR and marketing, while her husband is the manager. And his oldest daughter Terri is the dance instructor made famous for appearing in Queer Eye for the Straight Guy. Come in early Wednesday through Saturday and you can experience her infamous two-step lessons for yourself.

"People pay money to see the sideshow," says Stephanie. "She should take it on the road, is what I say."

Stephanie and her husband, musician Alvin Crow, are so integrated into the Spoke, they may as well be family. Alvin and James used to sing and roll a heavy wagon wheel around the bar together each night. A sign above the stage, added to celebrate 50 years of his playing on it, now reads "Home of Alvin Crow." He's also the one who got George Strait his first job at the Broken Spoke in 1975, and Strait went on to play there monthly for years.

James White's motto was "We're not changing nothin'"—and so they haven't, at least not cosmetically. Some other things, of course, had to change. For instance, beer was only a nickel when they opened, and a T-bone steak was $2.00. They also remained a beer-only, BYOB establishment until 1980. They still eschew a POS system for a calculator behind the bar, which is wild when you see how busy this nearly 700-person capacity place gets on the weekends. These days they serve draft Lone Star, canned and bottled beer and cider, plus all the spirits essential to well and basic call drinks. You won't find a cocktail menu here, but some of the regulars will order the drink James created, called, fittingly, The James: Deep Eddy Ruby Red grapefruit vodka with pineapple, cranberry, and a splash of Sprite.

The Spoke has been known for their chicken-fried steak through the years—and even featured on the Food Network for it at one point—but they have a full menu of items, from barbecue to Tex-Mex, and the same cook has been making it all for the last 24 years! Food can be enjoyed in the dancehall, or you can enjoy it out in the front bar before the party gets going. There's cozy booths, long tables for groups, pool tables, shuffleboard, and Jasper, their "night watchman" of a mannequin, originally added to the dining room after someone attempted to steal James White's father's saddle, which has since been recovered and lives behind a glass case. Between 6 and 8 p.m., there are free dinner shows in the front bar too, and it's a whole other, more intimate way to experience the Spoke.

There have been many rumors through the years about impending developments threatening The Broken Spoke's existence. And, with the little red shanty sandwiched between two looming condos, those rumors never seemed too far-fetched. However, they received some very good news on April 12, 2023, when the Spoke was recognized as a historical landmark by the state of Texas. And the fact that it happened on James White's birthday could lead one to believe that the honky-tonk hero is still keeping the bar's heart beating.

"It's very spiritual in here," says Stephanie. "Some people go to church to get the spirit, but I come here. I'd be here whether I worked here or not. It's a magnificent, beautiful, honest-to-goodness honky-tonk."

More Locally Loved South Lamar and South 1st Street Bars and Breweries:

HOUSE WINE
408 Josephine Street, Austin, TX 78704

GIBSON STREET BAR
1109 S Lamar Boulevard, Austin, TX 78704

THE BAR AT EL RAVAL
1500 S Lamar Boulevard, #150, Austin, TX 78704

UNDERDOG
1600 S. 1st Street, Austin, TX 78704

SAXON PUB
1320 S Lamar Boulevard, Austin, TX 78704

CORNER BAR
1901 S Lamar Boulevard, Austin, TX 78704

GOLDEN GOOSE
2034 S Lamar Boulevard, Austin, TX 78704

AUSTIN BEER GARDEN BREWING CO.
1305 W Oltorf Street, Austin, TX 78704

G & S LOUNGE
2420 S 1st Street, Austin, TX 78704

KELLY'S IRISH PUB
519 W Oltorf Street, Austin, TX 78704

BLACK SHEEP LODGE
2108 S Lamar Boulevard, Austin, TX 78704

AVIARY WINE & KITCHEN
2110 S Lamar Boulevard, Austin, TX 78704

EASY TIGER-SOUTH LAMAR
3508 S Lamar Boulevard, Suite 200, Austin, TX 78704

RADIO COFFEE & BEER
4204 Menchaca Road, Austin, TX 78704

SOUTH CONGRESS AND ST. EDWARD'S

Edwin Waller, Austin's first mayor, designed Congress Avenue to be one of Austin's most prominent thoroughfares in the 1800s. But it was the expansion of the streetcar down South Congress in the 1920s that spurred rapid growth. The Austin Motel opened in 1938, and the San José Motel followed shortly afterward. The legendary Continental Club opened its doors in 1955, initially as a supper club, then a burlesque club, and then a blue collar bar before it became a venue in the 1970s. The area became a destination for local artists and musicians, particularly after the opening of the nearby Armadillo World Headquarters in 1970 and Willie Nelson's Austin Opry House in 1977. By the 1980s, the area had fallen into disrepair, but new businesses moved in, attracted by the cheap rent. One was the iconic costume shop Lucy in Disguise, which opened in 1984, and 24-hour diner Magnolia Cafe, which opened on South Congress in 1988. An economic boom in the 1990s started to attract new residents. In 1995, Liz Lambert left her job at the attorney general's office to buy the San José Motel and transform it into a hip boutique hotel. She went on to become one of the city's most influential hoteliers, completing similar renovations on South Congress with the Austin Motel, Hotel Saint Cecilia, and Hotel Magdalena. Pretty soon, South Congress was a full-fledged tourist destination, but it still had that laid back, bohemian vibe for which the city is known. The street was lined with bookstores, vintage shops, clothing stores, restaurants, and eventually food trucks, and they all opened their doors in celebration of local community each first Thursday of the month. But then the inevitable happened: exorbitant rent increases forced local businesses to shut their doors or relocate. One by one, institutions like Uncommon Objects, Lucy in Disguise, Tesoros, and South Congress Books have disappeared and, in their place, corporations—like lululemon, Tuft & Needle, Nike, Madewell, and Hermès— have opened. There's even a Soho House.

But! One of the diviest karaoke bars of all time still exists at the bottom of South Congress, tucked in the parking garage of an office building, and that gives me hope. Ego's must be preserved at all costs. The Austin Motel's landmark neon sign always has a positive message on it and the historic hotel is now known for its inclusive, DJ-fueled pool parties. Continental Club and C-Boy's Heart & Soul (page 302) are doing their part to preserve and celebrate the Austin we know and love. The St. Edward's neighborhood has Cosmic Coffee + Beer Garden, a dog-friendly community space with a handful of food trucks plus coffee, cocktails, and beer. You can still visit the Cathedral of Junk and Casa Neverlandia, two large-scale home art projects created by local eccentrics, and I hope that never changes. And just south of Ben White, you'll find The Yard, an industrial warehouse complex housing St. Elmo Brewery, Still Austin distillery, Texas Saké Company, and The Austin Winery, each with its own incredible food truck.

EQUIPMENT ROOM

1101 Music Lane
Austin, TX 78704

Austin was dubbed the Live Music Capital of the World after it was discovered in the 1990s that the city had more live music venues per capita than anywhere else in the nation. But until recently, there was no place where an album was given the same respect and appreciation as, say, the food and drink. But in March of 2023, the city's first listening room opened inside the basement of the Hotel Magdalena. Equipment Room, which is located in a former space used to store equipment, is a collaboration between Bunkhouse hospitality group; Josh LaRue and Gabe Vaughn, the co-owners of Breakaway Records; and Mohawk owner James Moody. Inspired by the hi-fi vinyl bars of Japan known as kissas, Equipment Room is a place for audiophiles to hang out and appreciate records as they were intended to be heard, whether local folk from Cactus Lee or classic Coltrane. There are no DJs here, but rather curators of sound; albums are played all the way through, and if you inquire about a track, the equally passionate servers will scrawl the name of it onto a special card. The acoustic engineers at Klipsch helped design the space to have absolutely flawless sound. True to its name, the bar is stocked with hi-fi speakers and amplifiers, plus vintage 8-track and cassette players, and even stereo headphones that can be requested at the bar.

Behind the bar, around 1,200 LPs share space with a collection of spirits that leans heavy on the shōchū and Japanese whisky. The cocktail program, engineered by bar veteran Robert Björn Taylor, features A-Sides (classic drinks) and B-Sides (his take on the classics, all with music-inspired names). A Boulevardier A-Side yields an All Tomorrow's Parties B-side (Santa Teresa Solera 1796 rum, Batavia Arrack, Cynar, Giffard Banane Du Bresil), and a classic martini becomes an herbal, refreshing riff called Liquid Swords (Suntory Roku gin, Vermouth de Chambery Blanc, Junmai sake, gooseberries, cardamom bitters, black lemon bitters, and lemon oil). The succinct snack menu, from Hotel Magdalena's chef Jeffrey Hundelt, features well-done bites like tomato prosciutto toast, tuna onigiri, a tinned seafood board, and more.

The hall leading into the listening room is padded with egg crate foam, and I can't help but think that much of the incredible interior design also has sound in mind, from the thick velvet curtains sealing the space to the rounded corners of custom shelving holding vintage audio equipment, music books, and plants. The Japandi aesthetic is warm and unpretentious, with comfy, vintage-inspired couches, stained glass details, and chairs enhanced by pillows and sheepskin for added comfort. Framed vintage posters from legendary shows complete this living love letter to Austin music.

WATERTRADE

1603 S Congress Avenue
Austin, TX 78704

My favorite speakeasy in town isn't even a speakeasy at all. But it also doesn't have a Google listing. That's because Watertrade is technically a part of Otoko, the acclaimed omakase restaurant inside the South Congress Hotel. "It's the secret within the secret," says general manager Billy Weston. "They're separate but kind of the same." Both the bar and restaurant are accessed by a corten steel staircase in the hotel's courtyard. And once you ascend into the world of Watertrade, with its ambient lighting and vibey soundtrack, you know right away you are in for a treat.

You could sink into one of the buttery ribbed leather couches in the shadows or opt for a brighter nook, where vintage lounge chairs are divided by a screen and framed Japanese movie posters and Tokyo subway maps hang on the wall. But the best seats in the house are found at the bar, where the incredibly knowledgeable staff provide one of the most intimate cocktail experiences in town. Backlit bottles glow against the dark wooden back bar, which boasts the largest selection of Japanese whisky in the state, with around 140 different bottles.

"It's been a labor of love, making that happen," says Weston, who is incredibly humble about his staggering wealth of Japanese spirit knowledge. Here you'll find lesser known producers like Fukano Distillery, a shōchū and sake brewer who also specializes in barrel-aged,

koji-fermented rice whiskies, or Kaiyo, a distillery that keeps their quality high and prices low by growing and harvesting their own mizunara trees, the typical of oak responsible for giving Japanese whisky its sandalwood aromatics. They also maintain a collection of around 25 different types of shōchū, made from everything from carrot to sesame to Okanagan sugar cane.

"Shōchū as a category is still a little bit of a mystery to people, so I love talking about any and all of it to anyone who will listen," says Weston, citing Nishi Shuzo Tenshi, a very rare sherry barrel- aged shōchū, as his favorite. "There are more than 60 different botanicals you can make shōchū from…Rice shōchū is a good starter shōchū for those just starting to explore it. Sweet potato is funky, so you have to be ready to get weird." They also use the spirit to craft a complimentary welcome cocktail for all guests.

The bar is filled with a library of unlabeled bottles and dropper bottles of tinctures, bitters, and syrups, accentuated by a mirrored ceiling. And mushroom-shaped brass lamps on the bartop prove to be essential for reading the intricate, hand-sewn and illustrated cocktail menu. The inspiration for the latest program comes from sekki, the 24 microseasons used for agricultural purposes in Japan, similar to the Farmer's Almanac used in the West. Each cocktail plays off Japanese ingredients and flavors, and they work with the kitchen to utilize the Japanese practice of mottainai, or salvaging products that would otherwise go to waste. The Kanpachi Dirty is a complex, savory martini made with Tenshi No Yuwaku Imo shōchū, Dolin Dry, Dolin Blanc, 3 peppercorn tincture, kanpachi brine, and umami bitters. Yaeyama Baby! Is crafted from an umami-rich Wagyu fat-washed rum blend, Okinawan black sugar, ramp tincture, and black pepper, served with a bonito shortbread on the side.

There are about 50 sakes listed on the menu at any given time, but that's only half of what they stock. At the start of 2023, they unveiled their first private label sake, the samurai-inspired Revenge of the Third Son, a Junmai Daiginjo made from Yamada Nishiki rice. They created it in collaboration with Higashiyama Brewery, a brewery from chef Yoshi Okai's neighborhood in Kyoto.

Watertrade accepts walk-ins or reservations, and now offers an a la carte bar menu too, with dishes like eggplant fries, seasonally dressed oysters, caviar sets, crudos and binchotan grilled items…plus a hybrid mochi-churro miso ice cream sandwich I won't soon forget.

DAY IS NIGHT

Bar manager Nadia Hernandez created this cocktail based on Shūbun, the 16th sekki that bridges the gap between summer and fall. Whisky is lightened with the addition of awamori, Okinawa's indigenous distillate made from long grain rice and black koji, while Punt e Mes, epazote, and mushroom flavors layer herbaceousness, umami, and bitterness to create a harmonious blend of light and dark flavors. "The equinox is a time when the veil between the living and the dead thins and a time of opposites existing in harmonious balance, much like the disparate flavors and spirits in this cocktail," she says.

2 oz. Mars Iwai Tradition Whisky

½ oz. Shimauta awamori

½ oz. Punt e Mes

10 drops Epazote Tincture

10 drops Shiitake Mushroom Tincture

Luxardo cherry, to garnish

1. Add all ingredients to a mixing glass with ice and stir.
2. Strain into a coupe and garnish.

Epazote Tincture: Combine 5 g of fresh epazote leaves and 3 oz. of an overproof spirit (like Mohawk 190 Proof). Let the infusion steep for 48 hours in an airtight container. Strain and bottle.

Shiitake Mushroom Tincture: Spin 50 g of dehydrated shiitake mushrooms in a Vitamix on low. Add the spun chopped dehydrated mushrooms to an overproof spirit (like Mohawk 190 Proof) for two weeks, shaking regularly. Strain the shiitake mushrooms from the alcohol. Weigh out the amount of alcohol that remains and reserve an equal amount of water to be heated with. Add the water and soaked mushrooms, plus 50 more grams of dehydrated mushrooms, to a compression bag and vacuum seal. Sous vide for 4 hours at 160 degrees. Let cool, strain, and bottle.

JUNE'S ALL DAY

1722 S Congress Avenue
Austin, TX 78704

Austin has a patio culture that is widespread, year-round, and very distinctly... well, Austin. But the sidewalk patio outside June's All Day feels much more quaint and romantic: the umbrella-shaded marble tables, the woven French bistro chairs, the very European intimacy of the set-up on the corner of West Annie and South Congress. Order the moules frites and a glass of Chenin Blanc and you may just teleport straight to Paris.

June's isn't a French café, at least not strictly speaking. Restaurateur Larry McGuire took inspiration from several different concepts when fleshing this one out, and it shows in the diverse menu offerings. There's a touch of Spanish tapas bars, a dash of New York wine bars— and yes, a heavy dose of the Parisian cafes that appeal to tourists while also serving the neighborhoods they anchor.

"We wanted June's to be that place in Austin, definitely inspired by French café culture but unique to Travis Heights, where I grew up," says McGuire, who worked as a barista in the Texas French Bread that leased the space in this 100-year-old building when he was in high school. "The regulars from the surrounding neighborhoods, Bouldin Creek and Travis Heights, are the backbone of June's. We get plenty of visitors walking up and down South Congress, but it's the Austin folks, lifers and newly arrived ones, who make June's so special."

Now with over twenty bars and restaurants under his belt, each with its own distinct personality, you could say McGuire and his team at McGuire Moorman Lambert Hospitality, plus their constant collaborators at FÖDA design studio, have a knack for creating transportative spaces. The inside of June's is bright and airy during the day, with creamy marble bar tops, rattan barstools, green subway tiles, and black-and-white checkered floor tiles. A vintage jukebox and hi-fi sound system add to the café's timelessness. "Design-wise it has a patina to it that makes it feel like it's been there forever," says McGuire.

June's is named after June Rodil, the Master Sommelier who was leading MML Hospitality's beverage program when they opened in 2016. She has since departed to join Houston's Goodnight Hospitality as a partner, but her legacy carries on. The wine-focused menu attracts oenophiles from across the city to sip juice made with minimal intervention by well-respected producers like Heidi Schrock, Catherine and Pierre Breton, Mullineaux, and Bichi. June's quickly became an industry sweetheart for its Wine Blind tastings every Wednesday at noon. Those who can correctly guess the grape and region of four blind pours get them for free—or pay a minimal $10 otherwise. June's wine 'zine is another tradition that has carried on. Every couple months, they publish a 'zine with a different theme, highlighting offbeat and exceptional wines, regions, and producers.

In addition to a short weekday breakfast menu (featuring a breakfast chalupa and a Croque Madame), there's an all-day menu that's available whenever they're open, offering a little of everything, from a matzo ball caldo to a pastrami smoked salmon board to a spicy fried chicken sandwich. Every Sunday is Indian Pub Night, when they put out a menu of Indian curries with specials on pints of Old Speckled Hen.

OLIVE OIL MARTINI

Though wine is the focus at June's, the café has a short list of cocktails— and there's nothing more essential than an ice cold martini, especially with an order of the salt cod croquettes. At opening time, fat washing with spirits was becoming more and more popular so the bar team used extra virgin olive oil to elevate this simple classic while adding a textural richness and weight to the drink.

1 750-mL bottle Vodka OR 1 liter bottle London Dry Gin

½ cup Texas extra virgin olive oil

1 pitted Castelvetrano olive, to garnish

1. Combine the liquor and EVOO in a bottle and give the batch a brief stir to incorporate the flavors.

2. Let sit for 48 hours at room temperature and then freeze overnight.

3. Strain and discard leftover olive oil, then store the fat-washed liquor in the freezer.

4. Pour into a chilled martini glass and garnish with 1 pitted Castelvetrano olive.

C-BOY'S HEART & SOUL

2008 S Congress Avenue
Austin, TX 78704

Walking into C-Boy's Heart & Soul feels a bit like stumbling onto a movie set for a 1960s juke joint. It's sexy and moody, with red neon lights casting a glow across glossy black booths and high-top tables. A vintage Rowe AMI jukebox, though out of order, adds to the mise en scène, and behind the bar, a heart-shaped mirror lined in red and white lights also sets the tone. You can catch live music here seven days a week against a gold glittery stage backdrop. The focus here is on blues, soul, and R&B, from Rosie Flores to Jimmie Vaughn to Tomar and the FC's. And it's one of those places where it doesn't even matter if you know the artist or not. In fact, I'd recommend visiting as a way to discover new artists, because the music is always just that good.

And it's no wonder, because this bar is another brainchild of Steve Wertheimer, the proprietor of the famous Continental Club just down the street. It took Wertheimer a year of renovations to transform the former dive bar Trophy's (RIP) into C-Boy's in December of 2013, and the original sign can be seen in the back of the bar. The bar is named after L.C. "C-Boy" Parks, the beloved cook-turned-manager of the legendary campus-area Rome Inn back in the 1970s. Now the venue's old sign lives above the exit door at C-Boy's. Another absolute Austin treasure is the painting of Freddie King hanging on the wall above the jukebox. He riffs on the guitar while an armadillo bursts out of his chest like a heart. The illustrious artist Jim Franklin painted this to hang originally at the Armadillo World Headquarters, followed by Threadgill's, before it found a home here at C-Boy's.

Depending on the artist, the audience may stay seated, enjoying the show from dark, cozy booths. I've also been to high-energy shows where the crowd gathers under a disco ball at the front of the stage. I always seem to make fast friends with the folks on the patio, and I love slipping away to their second level Jade Room. Those in the know will head to the staircase on the outside of the south-facing wall, which leads up to another sultry, red-lit space. While C-Boy's downstairs is styled more for the early 1960s, the upstairs bar is one modeled after 1950s-era Japanese GI bars, with its Japanese beer and sake program, pin-up bar mirror, lotus-shaped pendant lights and Japanese-inspired wall decor.

So next time you head south on South Congress, look for the candy-striped awning, which pays homage to an early Continental Club entrance. Step inside and you'll very much feel like you've reached the heart and soul of the city.

More Locally Loved South Congress Bars:

EGO'S
510 S Congress Avenue, Austin, TX 78704

THE LOUNGE AT HOTEL SAN JOSE
1316 S Congress Avenue, Austin, TX 78704

THE CONTINENTAL CLUB & CONTINENTAL GALLERY
1315 S Congress Avenue, Austin, TX 78704

THE METEOR
2110 S Congress Avenue, Austin, TX 78704

More Locally Loved St. Edward's and East Congress Bars:

LITTLE DRINKS LOUNGE
3801 S Congress Avenue, Suite 116, Austin, TX 78704

COSMIC COFFEE + BEER GARDEN
121 Pickle Road, Austin, TX 78704

THE 04 LOUNGE
3808 S Congress Avenue, Austin, TX 78704

BENDER
321 W Ben White Boulevard, #300, Austin, TX 78704

STILL AUSTIN WHISKEY CO.
440 E St. Elmo Road, Suite F, Austin, TX 78745

TEXAS SAKÉ COMPANY
440 E St. Elmo Road, Suite B-2, Austin, TX 78745

SPOKESMAN-SOUTH
440 E St. Elmo Road, A2, Austin, TX 78745

THE AUSTIN WINERY
440 E St. Elmo Road, A1, Austin, TX 78745

RUSTY CANNON PUB
730 W. Stassney Lane, #120, Austin, TX 78745

SAGEBRUSH
5500 S Congress Avenue, Austin, TX 78745

WILLIAM CANNON, SLAUGHTER, AND MENCHACA

As central Austin becomes more congested—and expensive—folks are migrating south by the droves, especially those with young families. The neighborhoods between William Cannon and Slaughter offer slightly more affordable houses that were built in the 1970s and 1980s, as well as some more reasonable rates on newer apartment buildings. This wave of relocation has resulted in new businesses opening in South Austin, with plenty more to come. While there was already an abundance of old school Tex-Mex in South Austin, options for food are diversifying. The Little Darlin' (page 310) is a spacious family-friendly outdoor bar, with a stage and remarkably good food. The Thicket Food Park is a neighborhood hub filled with food trucks peddling Himalayan, Taiwanese, Israeli, Vietnamese, and more. South of Slaughter on Menchaca, there's an entire row of beer gardens and bars, seemingly built for the masses and all offering different food truck options. Golden Hour is bringing natural wine and European-inspired bar bites to the southern 'burbs and, further east, Ramen Tatsu-ya has expanded to a far South location right near the Far Out Lounge (page 313). A cluster of breweries has opened in the industrial area surrounding I-35, and further east near 71 and Burleson, Meanwhile Brewing has become an extremely popular spot for young families.

THE LITTLE DARLIN'

6507 Circle S Road
Austin, TX 78745

It is quite rare to find a bar that is also a venue...where the drinks are good, the prices are fair— and they serve delicious food too? Somehow, The Little Darlin' is doing it all, and they're doing it well. That's just a testament to the magic that can happen when close friends discover they are great business partners too. In 2016, Mimi and Brian Buscemi teamed up with Mike and Karinne Sanchez to open up The Little Darlin' off of East William Cannon Road, just west of I-35. The property was originally a home, built in 1957, where Lula and Gilbert Lafuente opened La Fuente's Tex-Mex restaurant in 1969. The restaurant was passed down to their kids, then sold to a couple local investors who ran it until 2015.

"The plank wood ceiling may have given us some motivation to carry on the theme," remembers Mimi. "As you can imagine, a limited budget called for all the more creativity." They brought on a couple of carpenter friends, and one had access to a considerable amount of reclaimed wood which they used to craft tables, chairs, and booths for the interior. They painted the walls bright red to match the red felted pool tables. Brian crafted rustic wall sconces using materials he found in his garage. "And I think we could make the case that the mounted Slayer poster printed in pig's blood and

our beloved photo print of Gibby Haynes, Willie Nelson, and Roky Erickson is a good introduction to who we, as owners, are," says Mimi.

The Little Darlin' is like a slightly grown-up version of Yellow Jacket (page 141), where Mimi is also a partner. It has all the creature comforts you care more about when you get a little more… discerning. You know: parking, space, plenty of comfy seats—once, I sat and comfortably ate soup while watching a Dead Prez show, if that helps paint a picture. It's dog and kid-friendly, with an expansive shade-covered backyard scattered with picnic tables, porch swings, horseshoes, and washers.

"It's a nod to old Austin," says Karinne. "A comfortable space to which you could bring a date, pals, grandparents—with everything from Kitty Wells to Iron Maiden playing overhead."

The Little Darlin' also features a dozen rotating beers on tap, and they make housemade infusions, like strawberry chili mango vodka, walnut bourbon, Best Maid pickles with vodka, grilled pineapple-jalapeño tequila, 8 pepper vodka, and seasonal flavors. They then build simple cocktails using those infusions. They also get agua fresca mixes every few days from their friends at Lula's Aguas to craft their popular daily frozen agua fresca, made with tequila. The food here is exceptional, and goes well above and beyond bar food offerings: sirloin steak salad, carnitas sliders, kale caesar salad, chorizo tempeh burgers, apple-stuffed pork loin with smoked gouda grits and collard greens.They also offer a daily seafood special, which could be a cedar smoked salmon salad with green goddess dressing or fried catfish and slaw or Peruvian mahi with yucca fries and cabbage salad.

The owners all grew up in the punk scene as teens and have lots of relationships in the music world, from working at venues to watching friends become accomplished musicians or started their own agencies. As such, music is a huge part of The Little Darlin', and they regularly host free shows. Artists that have graced their stage include Roky Erickson, Peelander-Z, Del The Funky Homosapien, Grupo Fantasma, Kool Keith, Fuckemos, Dale Watson, and Bun B with UGK. They also host daytime family-friendly shows and events, doggie costume contests, drag brunches, pop-up markets, fundraisers, and more.

"We wanted to make a space we, as owners, genuinely enjoy spending time in, and of course, share that," says Karinne. "With the evolution of the city, I feel like our intention to carve out a pocket of this town and preserve a little bit of the special culture we grew up with—by bringing together good folks, over good food and drinks —can be felt. At least, I hope!"

THE FAR OUT LOUNGE

8504 S Congress Avenue
Austin, TX 78745

The little stone cottage now housing The Far Out Lounge on far South Congress has seen a lot. It was built in 1908 and, for a period of time, it was called The Last Chance bar because it was thought of as "the last change to get a beer before San Antonio." In the 1920s, the outlaw Newton Boys used the structure as a hideout after bank and train heists. Janis Joplin played here when she was still just a student at UT. From 1980 to 2008, it was a biker bar called Beverly's, and they hosted toy drives for kids in need each summer. During that time, it also served as the set for outlaw movies like *Pair of Aces* (1990) starring Kris Kristofferson and Willie Nelson, and *Nadine* (1987), starring Jeff Bridges and Kim Basinger. From 2009 to 2019, it was a divey bar called the Red Shed until the owners decided to shutter it, at which point Bay Anthon and Pedro Carvalho jumped on the opportunity for the space.

"The Far Out was a dream project that started at Hopfields," remembers Carvalho. "I was the General Manager working under Bay Anthon and our love for live music, great drinks and the experiences of living in Austin led us down the colorful rainbow that is The Far Out."

They originally opened in 2019 as a cocktail bar called Nicolaza's, with a Hopfields sibling food truck out-

side, but decided to rebrand as an actual venue in late summer 2019. No sooner had TFO been voted Best New Music Venue by The Austin Chronicle then the pandemic caused everything to shut down. "In some sense, I still feel like we are in the opening stages since the last two years have been so crazy," says Carvalho.

Despite that uncertain start, the bar—and the sprawling 3 acres it's set on—is filled with life again, and hosting some sort of event just about every day. The venue is home to the annual Hot Sauce Fest, has hosted Lone Star Zine Fest, and has been the site of reunion shows and revivals like Woodshock 2022, I Still Miss Liberty

Lunch Reunion, Bikini Kill, and Austin Psych Fest. And that's in addition to regular vintage markets, fundraisers, bike meet-ups, film screenings, art shows, music and wine pairings—you name it and it has probably been done at The Far Out, even in its short lifetime.

The spacious backyard is shaded by live oaks, draped with twinkling lights and scattered with oilcloth-lined picnic tables and prickly pear cacti. A bright yellow barn structure features a colorful monster mural painted by local artist Jeff Skele, and the doors open to reveal the stage. Most of the shows I've seen here have been illuminated by a spectrum of liquid lights or other psychedelic projections, which spread onto the trees around the stage for an extra magical effect.

Carvalho says their inspiration for TFO was, "Austin and its vibrant art and music scene. We wanted to capture the true essence of what it meant to live in South Austin's music scene. 1970s psychedelic color patterns on the walls, tons of purples, graffiti murals curated by local artists that we love, and a festival scene curated by some of our favorite artisanal vendors."

The inside bar—with its little lounge of mismatched vintage furniture, fire engine red walls and plants—has the laid-back feel of a welcoming house party. A very cool thing that they do is commission artists like Grace Reyer, Billie Buck and Fez Moreno to design a poster for every show that takes place, and the framed pieces line the walls and cover the bathrooms too. I have a feeling we'll be seeing these posters for years to come, sold as vintage collectibles.

A groovy purple, red, and gold design behind the bar pulls the bar's theme colors together, and greenery spills out of the gold geometric shelving over the bar. There are 48 taps between the inside and outside bar, with a huge selection of craft beer. The spirits collection has a focus on tequila and whiskey and they feature rotating cocktail specials like elderflower lemonade and hibiscus palomas. The all-time favorite is the draft spicy margarita, a blend of mezcal, tequila, Ancho Reyes with a Tajín rim. In true Austin spirit, the patio is dog-friendly, the prices are reasonable, and there's food trailer options.

Now, if you don't already live South, TFO is both kinds of far out.. but well worth the trek. Just look for the reader board blinking "South Austin Forever."

SMOKY MARGARITA

The Far Out's first draft cocktail, the Smoky Margarita, was created by then-bartender, now-manager, Clayton England. The drink was designed to embrace the level of increasing volume while keeping true to the bar's roots located in South Austin's fastest growing area. "While mezcal margaritas continue to grow in popularity in central Texas, the palate of mezcal can often be surprising and frankly off-putting to the unexpected drinker from out of town," says England. "The Smoky Margarita, a beautifully and simply balanced take on a staple cocktail, lets visitors and neighbors alike know exactly where they're at."

1 oz. silver tequila

½ oz. mezcal

1 oz. fresh lime juice

1 oz. triple sec

¼ oz. Ancho Verde poblano liqueur

Tajín and salt, to garnish (optional)

1. Combine all ingredients in a shaker over fresh ice, then shake until your arm hurts.
2. For a real South Austin feel, rim the glass with salt and Tajín.
3. Strain over fresh ice in glass and garnish with a lime.

SAM'S TOWN POINT

2115 Allred Drive
Austin, TX 78748

There are very few places in Austin that feel entirely untouched by change, and Sam's Town Point is one of them. Its discreet location surely has something to do with it. The little beige lean-to with a corrugated metal roof is tucked into a neighborhood behind Slaughter and Manchaca, and the "sign" is a rusty pole out front... missing the sign itself. "You kind of have to get lost to find us," says owner Ramsay Midwood.

In 1979, Penny Grossman left Chicago for Austin, with a dream of opening a dance hall. She purchased a rural 4-acre plot near Slaughter and Manchaca and opened the bar two years later. The city limits used to run right through the property, so the parking lot was in Austin and the bar was in Travis County. Grossman wanted Sam, her old boss and investor back in Chicago, to know that there was a dance club for him to visit and it was located at the southernmost point of town. And so Sam's Town Point was born: part honky-tonk and part backwoods roadhouse, with a touch of David Lynch. Its red-curtained stage has hosted a cornucopia of different music styles, from outlaw country and Western swing to Cajun, blues, lounge and soul. Both Shinyribs and Mike and the Moonpies played their first shows here, and gonzo-songwriter Kinky Friedman makes regular appearances on this stage too. There's live music

every night of the week, with two shows on Fridays and Saturdays, and Double or Nothing Two Step hosts dance lessons every Thursday night.

Midwood is a singer-songwriter who played his first show at Sam's in 2002, soon after he'd moved to town. He immediately fell in love with the place, and Grossman with his music, and went on to lead the house band, backed by a rotating cast of Austin musicians. Over the next two decades, he became a part of the Sam's Town Point family, booking shows and helping out wherever needed. When Grossman tragically lost her son in a motorcycle accident and decided to retire in 2017, Midwood took over and continues to carry on her legacy. And Grossman, who still lives on the property, is there almost every night, enjoying the music while she holds court in her designated chair at the end of the bar.

Sam's has historically been a beer bar that sold set-ups and allowed guests to bring their own liquor, but Midwood secured a liquor license for the first time right before the pandemic. Now you can order a rum-based Yacht Rock Punch or a lavender whiskey sour from the long wooden bar, which is lined with vintage Budweiser ads and lit by a Clydesdale carousel lamp. If you're lucky, you'll catch Cathy Guthrie (yes, that Guthrie) behind the bar. She's one half of the folk-comedy duo Folk Uke with Amy Nelson (yes, that Nelson), and they'll play at Sam's every now and then too.

Aesthetically, the place hasn't changed much at all through the years which, of course, is part of the charm. Wood-paneled walls meet crackly acoustic ceiling tiles and bead curtains lead to the bathroom. A vintage Lone Star lamp illuminates the beige-felted pool table. The wooden dance floor, polished by happy feet through the years, runs right up to the original teal carpeting. The furniture is a mix of red cushioned captain's armchairs, a well-worn couch, and 1980s cinema seats. Neon and vintage beer signs make up the majority of the wall decor, but you'll also find taxidermy lit by laser lights, or maybe a rogue mannequin head. It's like the Regal Beagle on psychedelics. "No TVs—just live music and tasteless jokes," says Midwood.

The audience is just as eclectic. Sam's attracts a mix of hippies and cowboys, veterans and college kids, regulars and newbies— and they all commingle on the tree-shaded outdoor patio, a patchwork of mismatched tables and chairs, fire pits and an outdoor stage, illuminated by strands of lights and an oak-suspended chandelier. A motley cast of characters frequent the place and all pitch in to help it run, and Penny's daughter Diane will occasionally grill burgers and fries, adding to the backyard barbecue feel of the place. Most recently, Capital Taco joined the party, now serving tacos, quesadillas, fajitas, and queso to anyone who's danced up an appetite.

Sam's may be a venue, but it's so much more than that. Once you've found yourself there, you should plan to stick around and stay awhile. After all, as the sign in large print above the exit reminds us, "Friends Are the Best Part of Life"—and you're bound to make a few here.

GIDDY UPS

12010 Menchaca Road
Austin, TX 78748

Now, if anyone has seen some extreme changes take place surrounding their bar, it's Nancy Morgan. The 70-year-old bar owner can remember when Giddy Ups sat on 6 acres of rural land on Menchaca Road— and before 600 apartments were built on 4 of those acres. "We were out in the boonies," she remembers. "Across the road, where the storage place is now, was a beautiful cattle ranch that used to have calf roping and events there. I have had customers ride their horse to the bar and home again. A few times there were real, live horses inside the bar, just hanging out."

Samuel Dodson built the bar out of cement blocks in the 1950s and named it Dodson's. Back then, the area south of Slaughter Lane was settled by Black families. The Dodson family owned 10 acres and farmed the area, growing vegetables and butchering hogs. After it became Giddy Ups in 1993, Morgan added a patio and fireplace, before changing the bar's plain white exterior into a bright red Western saloon-inspired facade. The front of the bar is wrapped in license plates Morgan has collected over the years, or guests have donated. And the bar top is a whole mesquite trunk she found in Burnet and had friends help her finish and install.

In those early days, before the subdivisions were built, she remembers hosting turkey shoots, dove hunts, clay pigeon practice, hayrides, and bonfires. Each year, the bar put on a chili cookoff to raise money for various charities, and they hosted a big drive for children's toys every Christmas. In 2007, she hired a regular—who was also a booker—to teach her how to book music, and she turned the bar into a venue as well. The walls with framed posters from past shows lining the wall: Murali Coryell, W.C. Fields, Choctaw Wildfire, the late James Hand.

These days, they still host live music five days a week, with karaoke and open mic on the other nights, and Morgan still vets new bands by watching them play elsewhere ahead of time. "It was a ton of work, and I still do this," she says. "I do not book a band unless I've seen them play live somewhere. Then I can see how they interact with the crowd, how loud they are—many different things go into booking an act at Giddy Ups."

In addition to a wide variety of beer, Giddy Ups serves some simple mixed drinks with honky-tonk inspired names, like Boots & Spurs, and they also offer several different flights of whiskey, which is a focus of the spirits program. Adjacent to the bar's interior is a spacious outdoor bar area with garage doors on both ends and a shuffleboard centerpiece. There's also a sign listing the bar rules: Respect Yourself, Respect Each Other and Respect the Property. Morgan remembers when it used to be a rough and tumble bar, and she'd have to ask people to "take it outside." "I would get them to go out back to fight and not tear up the bar. They would go fists to cuffs and then come in clean up and buy each other a beer. Life was simpler then — no knives, guns and deadly violence, just good old fashioned fist fights and still be friends."

Morgan said she's lost some of her favorite old timers in recent years— like Lester Shiller, who used to play pool with the handle end of a broom stick, and win every single time, to the dismay of whatever newbie was playing him. Now that younger patrons are coming in, Morgan is schooling them on her zero policy tolerance for rude or obnoxious behavior, and she's become known as Mom to some.

"Sometimes when we have younger folks come in and they start to act up , I just say, "Hey, would you act like that in your Mom's living room? This is my living room and you cannot act like that here!'" she says. "This is a safe place. People come back again and again, and have made friends for life over the years."

More Locally Loved William Cannon, Slaughter, and Menchaca Bars:

GOLDEN HOUR CAFE & WINE BAR
7731 Menchaca Road, Suite 100, Austin, TX 78745

ARMADILLO DEN
10106 Menchaca Road, Austin, TX 78748

MOONTOWER SALOON
10212 Menchaca Road, Austin, TX 78748

LULU'S
10402 Menchaca Road, Building C, Austin, TX 78748

SOUTH AUSTIN BEER GARDEN
10700 Menchaca Road, Austin, TX 78748

Locally Loved South Austin Breweries & Cideries:

MEANWHILE BREWING
3901 Promontory Point Drive, Austin, TX 78744

PINTHOUSE BREWING
2202 E Ben White Boulevard, Austin, TX 78741

NOMADIC BEERWORKS
3804 Woodbury Drive, Suite A, Austin, TX 78704

(512) BREWING COMPANY
407 Radam Lane, Austin, TX 78745

ST. ELMO BREWING COMPANY
440 E St. Elmo Road, G-2, Austin, TX 78745

VACANCY BREWING
415 E St. Elmo Road, 1 D2, Austin, TX 78745

LAST STAND BREWING COMPANY
7601 S Congress Avenue, Building 6, Austin, TX 78745

THIRSTY PLANET BREWING COMPANY
8201 S Congress Avenue, Austin, TX 78745

TEXAS KEEPER CIDER
12521 Twin Creek Road, Manchaca, TX 78652

SUDS MONKEY BREWING CO.
12024 US-290, Austin, TX 78737

JESTER KING BREWERY
13187 Fitzhugh Road, Austin, TX 78736

BEERBURG BREWING
13476 Fitzhugh Road, Austin, TX 78736

About the Author

Veronica Meewes lives in Austin, Texas, where she writes about food, beverage, travel and lifestyle. Her work has appeared in *Forbes Travel Guide*, *Food & Wine*, *Texas Monthly*, *Tasting Table*, *GOOD*, *PUNCH*, *The Today Show*, *The Local Palate*, *Cosmopolitan*, *Vera*, *Serious Eats*, *EatingWell*, *Austin Monthly*, *Fodor's*, *Vinepair*, *Texas Highways*, and more. When she's not seeking out the best food and drink around the globe, you can find her hiking, swimming, doing yoga, enjoying all the live music Austin has to offer, and exploring with her pup Banjo.

veronicameewes.com

About Cider Mill Press
Book Publishers

Good ideas ripen with time. From seed to harvest,
Cider Mill Press strives to bring fine reading,
information, and entertainment together between
the covers of its creatively crafted books. Our Cider
Mill bears fruit twice a year, publishing a new crop of
titles each spring and fall.

"Where good books are ready for press"
501 Nelson Place
Nashville, Tennessee 37214

cidermillpress.com